Techniques in Inventory Management and Control

By

Charles D. Mecimore, Ph.D., CPA, CMA
Professor of Accounting
The University of North Carolina at Greensboro

James K. Weeks, Ph.D.
Associate Professor of Information Systems
and Operations Management
The University of North Carolina at Greensboro

A study carried out on behalf of the
National Association of Accountants
Montvale, New Jersey

Published by

National Association of Accountants
10 Paragon Drive
Montvale, NJ 07645-1760
Mandel & Wagreich, Inc., Cover

NAA Publication Number 86192
ISBN 0-86641-152-6

Foreword

In 1964 the National Association of Accountants published Research Report 40, *Research in Inventory Management*. Since that time, several events have had a direct impact on the management of inventory. Some of the more noted occurrences are:

1. The computer has become widely applied in inventory management.
2. Material Requirements Planning (MRP) has been developed and installed in many manufacturing concerns.
3. Foreign competitors, particularly the Japanese, have successfully implemented innovative inventory management approaches. An outgrowth of this success and increased competition has been the wide adoption of the Just-in-Time/Zero Inventory approach.
4. The concept of management accounting responsibility has changed, and in some companies individuals in these positions are actively involved in the design and implementation of computerized inventory management systems.

These changes have made the 1964 report outdated and have emphasized the need for a more current presentation of inventory management techniques — the subject of this new research report requested by NAA's Committee on Research.

Presented here are the results of field studies of manufacturing and nonmanufacturing firms. It was surprising to find a relatively infrequent use of quantitative models to supplement experience-based decision making despite computer technology advances in inventory management information systems. Basic inventory concepts such as the establishment of service-level policies and balancing stockout costs are not being used frequently in making inventory decisions. Furthermore, more than 85% of the respondents indicated no plans to change their inventory mangement systems, undoubtedly reflecting the high financial and organizational costs necessary to make such changes — particularly so for those who have already adopted MRP and other computerized systems.

Other findings indicate that:

1. Turnover ratios and the calculation of dollars of obsolete inventory are popular methods employed to evaluate inventory effectiveness, and
2. New inventory systems, such as Just-in-Time, are being implemented without the development of supporting financial and accounting systems.

Traditional cost accounting systems will have to be modified and/or replaced so accounting departments can cope within these new environments.

Guidance in the preparation of this research report was kindly provided by the Project Committee:

David W. Vogel, *Chairman*
E. I. DuPont de Nemours & Co.
Wilmington, Delaware

Gail W. DeLong   Arjan T. Sadwani
Develco   University of Akron
San Diego, California   Akron, Ohio

The report reflects the views of the researchers and not necessarily those of the Association, the Committee on Research, or the Project Committee.

Patrick L. Romano
Director of Research
National Association of Accountants

Acknowledgments

We would like to extend our thanks to several people who provided assistance in the completion of this project. The authors are grateful for the support of the NAA Research Committee and for the guidance provided by the Project Committee members. In particular, we would like to thank David W. Vogel, chairman of the Project Committee, and Patrick Romano, NAA director of research, for their continued support and encouragement. Steven Landekich, former NAA director of research, and Willard Cox, former Project Commitee chairman are also to be commended for their counsel and advice during the earlier stages of the study.

This study would not have been possible without the time and cooperation of the many individuals who completed the questionnaires, many with extensive remarks attached, and those who were helpful in the telephone follow-up conversations. We thank these people for giving so much of their time.

Finally, we would like to express our appreciation to Barbara Mecimore for editorial and typing support and to Kent Slemmons for the many hours spent in data analysis.

Charles D. Mecimore
James K. Weeks

About the Authors

Charles D. Mecimore

Charles D. Mecimore, CMA, is professor and head of the Department of Accounting at the University of North Carolina at Greensboro. A CPA in North Carolina and Ohio, Dr. Mecimore holds a Ph.D. from the University of Alabama, an M.S. degree from the University of North Carolina at Chapel Hill, and a B.S. degree from Pfeiffer College. He received the Robert Beyer Bronze Medal for the third-highest scores on the 1975 CMA exam. In 1985 he received the Outstanding Educator Award from the North Carolina Association of CPAs.

A past national director of NAA, Dr. Mecimore has served as a chapter president and has been a member of several national committees.

James K. Weeks

James K. Weeks is associate professor of Information Systems and Operations Management at the School of Business and Economics at the University of North Carolina at Greensboro where he teaches graduate and undergraduate courses in production/operations management. He received a Ph.D. degree in business administration from the University of South Carolina. Dr. Weeks has published numerous articles in the areas of job shop scheduling, inventory management, production and operation management, process planning, and decision theory. He is a member of and has held a variety of leadership positions in several national and regional professional organizations. Dr. Weeks has presented numerous papers and speeches at conferences of these professional organizations. He also has been active in production management development seminars for a variety of firms including IBM, Rockwell International, Ciba-Geigy, E.I. DuPont de Nemours & Co., and Gulf-Western.

Table of Contents

Chapter 1

Introduction

In 1964, the National Association of Accountants published Research Report 40, *Techniques in Inventory Management.* Since that time, several events have occurred that have had a direct impact on the management of inventory. Some of the more notable occurrences are:

1. The computer has been widely applied in inventory management.
2. Materials Requirements Planning (MRP) has been developed and installed in many manufacturing companies.
3. Foreign competition, particularly from the Japanese, has successfully implemented innovative inventory management approaches. The Just-In-Time/Zero Inventory approach has been widely adopted in the United States.
4. The concept of management accounting responsibility has changed and in some companies individuals responsible for management accounting are actively involved in the design and implementation of computerized inventory management systems.

These changes make the 1964 report on inventory management obsolete. The objective of this report is to provide a more current presentation of inventory management techniques and applications. Field studies of manufacturing and nonmanufacturing firms were conducted to provide insight on the state of current inventory management practices.

Field Studies

Two field studies were conducted. The first, a general survey of inventory management practices, was conducted with a reference

1

group of 351 accountants divided into two groups: manufacturing and nonmanufacturing. Accountants, as opposed to inventory managers, were selected for the following reasons:

1. One of the objectives of this report was to survey accountants for their perception of the state of inventory management in their companies.

2. Inventory management and control has traditionally been an area of concern for management accounting, and, presumably, accountants would know about current practices in their firm.

3. The reference group of accountants was an easily identifiable and available sample of respondents who should have an interest in the topic.

The general survey of accountants and their response rates are shown in Exhibit 1-1. A copy of the general survey questionnaire, with the tabulated answers to each question, is included as Appendix A.

Exhibit 1-1
General Survey Questionnaire Response

Group	Number Surveyed	Usable Responses	% Responses
Plant Accountants-Manufacturing	206	57	27.7%
Controllers-Nonmanufacturing	145	31	21.4
	351	88	25.1%

Data from the 88 usable responses were coded and analyzed. Results from this analysis are included in the related chapters of the research report. General summaries and conclusions are presented later in this chapter.

While these data were being analyzed, and after reviewing the current literature, it became apparent that a rather new philosophy of inventory management was being considered and implemented. Originating with Japanese companies, the Just-In-Time/Zero Inventory management philosophy or approach was being installed in many manufacturing companies. A second, more specific, questionnaire was designed to survey firms on the extent of JIT/ZI implementations. Two hundred twenty-five manufacturing companies were surveyed. Those surveyed included three groups. These groups, the number of companies surveyed, and the number of usable responses are shown in Exhibit 1-2. Seventeen companies who had been reported in inventory management publications to have successful JIT/ZI implementations, a random sample of 194 plant accountants, and 14 companies, that responded to the first survey, and indicated that they would participate in follow-up interviews were surveyed. A copy of the questionnaire, with the responses to each question tabulated, is included as Appendix B. These data and the implications indicated by the responses are presented in Chapter 7.

Exhibit 1-2
Just-In-Time Survey Questionnaire Response

Group	Number Surveyed	Usable Responses	% Responses
Companies with JIT Systems	17	7	41.2%
Random Sample of Plant Accountants	194	63	32.5
Companies Included in First Questionnaire	14	7	50.0
	225	77	34.2%

More than 20% of the plant accountant respondents indicated their firm was considering or had adopted JIT/ZI systems. Because these systems have far-reaching impact on manufacturing systems and, indirectly, on the cost accounting systems of these companies, the potential impact of JIT/ZI for accountants is explored in Chapter 8.

Telephone Interviews

Follow-up telephone interviews with selected respondents of both studies were conducted to verify the data, to clarify responses, and to supplement these responses with additional information. These interviews were a valuable source of information in preparing this report and the authors wish to extend special thanks to those individuals who participated in these interviews.

Survey Results

Survey results indicate that experience is used much more frequently than quantitative models to manage inventories. What is surprising is the relative infrequency of quantitative models being used to supplement experience-based decision making. A minority of firms seem to be relying strictly on quantitative models, while others rely strictly on experience or a combination of experience and models. The relative infrequency of use of quantitative models indicates that the advances in inventory theory over the past 30 years have been applied unevenly in industry.

Except for finished goods (or merchandise) inventories, relatively few firms use service-level policies or base these policies on balancing stockout and carrying costs when deciding when to reorder. Many, if not most, of the companies use experience and intuition, which may be inferior when compared to statistical methods in setting safety stock levels. Experience rarely reflects the interrelated effects of forecast errors on desired safety stock levels, lead time variations, order quantity size, and desired service levels.

Time-phased ordering approaches, including Materials Requirements Planning (MRP) and Distribution Requirements Planning (DRP), are the most frequently used inventory management systems. These systems are found in more than 72% of the manufacturing and in more than 48% of the nonmanufacturing respondents. Fixed time period systems are used at no more than one out of 10 responding firms. Fixed order quantity systems are used to some extent but not nearly as much as the volume of inventory theory would indicate.

MRP/DRP systems are designed to manage inventory in dependent demand environments. These systems have been developed since the original NAA research report on inventory management and have been one of the most popular topics in production and inventory management over the past decade. During this period, the definition of these systems has evolved from a narrow focus on exploding material requirements to a business planning focus on integrating all functional units in the organization.

The number of successful MRP/DRP implementations is a surprisingly small percentage of the large and increasing number of implementation attempts over the past decade. The major obstacle to successful implementation has not been technical problems such as record accuracy but instead has been the difficulties of overcoming resistance to change.

The survey results indicate that about 70% of the respondents use some type of MRP/DRP system to manage their inventories. Most of these systems are first-generation systems and relatively few are

"Class A" systems. More than 85% of the respondents indicated no plans to change their inventory management system, undoubtedly reflecting their desire to improve and refine systems that have had high financial and organizational costs.

Weekly time periods ("buckets") for planning and weekly review periods are used by more than 65% of the respondents. Full regeneration was reported by more than 66% of the manufacturing respondents, while more than 75% of the nonmanufacturing respondents reported the net change method. The lot-for-lot and economic order quantity rules were reported by more than 68% of the respondents. Safety stocks are most frequently carried at the raw materials and finished goods levels.

Inventory management information systems have changed dramatically since the 1964 research report. Historically, these systems have been manual, informal systems. Computer-related technology advances in performance and costs and increased market competition have forced most companies to computerize some, if not most, of their inventory management information systems. Survey results indicate the subsystems of this information system that are most frequently computerized include bill of materials, materials requirement planning, master scheduling, cost accounting, general ledger accounting, and transaction history. Software programs for these subsystems are most frequently designed in-house on a modular basis.

Management must be concerned with control as well as with the effective and efficient use of the investment in inventory. Two useful techniques for identifying and monitoring inventory items are cycle counting and ABC analysis. These techniques may be employed most frequently where it is not feasible to look at each item in the inventory because of the cost involved in such a task. They allow management to focus on those items where the potential for large savings in inventory costs exists.

Two methods of evaluating existing inventory system effectiveness are found in practice. One method relies on ratios, while the other calculates dollar amounts. Based upon an analysis of responses to the questionnaire used in this study, turnover ratios are the most popular method of performance measurement. The second most popular tool is calculation of dollars of obsolete inventory. Each compares actual data with standards derived primarily from past experience.

Just-In-Time/Zero Inventory is a relatively new approach to

managing inventories. While its focus is on reducing inventories to zero levels, the underlying philosophy is to get rid of all wastes in the system. Thus, it is more than an inventory management approach; it is a total system management approach. The results of a survey of JIT/ZI users indicates these are relatively new programs in most firms, and they are viewed as total system programs that are strategically important to the firm. Because of this, top management leadership and support, primarily in the form of education and training, are viewed as the most critical factors of success. Dramatic improvements in performance, particularly in work-in-process (WIP) and raw materials inventory levels, are reported. These systems are being implemented without the development of supporting financial and accounting systems.

Implementing JIT/ZI inventory systems in a manufacturing environment almost certainly means major changes throughout a company. Many of those changes impact on the cost accounting systems currently in place. Some of the more obvious difficulties with traditional cost accounting systems in JIT/ZI environments are identified, along with some of the questions that must be answered before managerially meaningful cost systems may be developed. Because the JIT/ZI systems are just now being implemented in this country, the full impact of such systems on the accounting function is yet to be determined.

Summary and Conclusions

The survey results indicate that relatively few firms use quantitative models to decide when and how much to order. Most manufacturing firms use computer-based MRP systems, but only a small percentage of these users have "Class A" systems. Just-In-Time/Zero Inventory (JIT/ZI) systems have been installed in many firms, and many more are considering implementing these systems. Plant accountants are largely unaware of these systems, and the current cost accounting systems are lacking from an inventory management perspective in JIT/ZI environments.

Chapter 2

Inventory Functions, Costs, and Order Quantity Decision Approaches

The office manager of St. Pius Catholic Church has just completed a monthly review of supplies and decides to order candles. An inventory manager of ABC Tooling receives a memo that there are technical problems in the field with the gear boxes produced for a U.S. Department of Defense contract and decides not to order any more. A store clerk at a supermarket receives a stock authorization list from a computer terminal in the storage room and immediately withdraws the indicated quantities of the various items and places them on the shelf. Activities such as the ones cited above are played out daily in virtually every organization in our economic system. The common thread of these activities is a concern for managing inventory levels. Managing inventories revolves around two decisions: how much to order and when to order. In this chapter, the characteristics, functions, and costs of inventories are examined and used as the foundation for presenting alternative decision models for the "How much to order?" question. In Chapter 3, various approaches for answering the "When to order?" question are presented.

Definitions and Characteristics

Inventories may be viewed as stores of those items, materials, goods, and services required to carry on normal operations, or to meet normal sales expectations. Inventories include all materials that are required in the production and/or distribution processes as well as those necessary in the normal business flow of retail, financial, and other types of operations. Inventories can be classified according to their condition or degree of completion in meeting customer demand.

1. Finished goods (merchandise inventory) — items ready for sale and delivery to a customer.

7

2. Components — parts or subassemblies ready to go into the final assembly of finished goods.
3. Work in process — materials, components, and parts being worked on in a manufacturing environment.
4. Raw materials — items purchased and used to make the components of finished goods.

Organizations also inventory supplies or those material costs not normally identified as part of finished goods costs.

The relative importance of these types of inventories depends upon the nature of the operation. Product-oriented manufacturing organizations experience more inventory situations than do service organizations. Make-to-stock manufacturers must manage and interrelate finished goods, work-in-process, and raw materials. Make-to-order manufacturers have little or no finished goods inventories but usually have considerable inventories of raw materials and work-in-process. Wholesalers and retailers have only finished goods merchandise inventory. In service industries, such as hospitals, laundries, and food services, the only inventories of concern are purchased materials. In legal and educational services, supplies may be the only meaningful inventory to be managed.

However, all inventories share the following common characteristics:

1. Inventories represent a financial investment for the company.
2. Inventories become part of the cost of goods sold and are, therefore, a business expense.
3. Inventories use storage space, require handling, incur taxes, require insurance, and sometimes deteriorate, become obsolete, or get lost or stolen.
4. The availability of the right item at the right time is necessary for operating any production process or satisfying a demand by a customer for a finished product.
5. Inventories are not self-correcting--they must be managed, and effective management requires appropriate measures of performance.

All profit-oriented organizations carry inventory with these characteristics. Many are facing environments that are increasingly competitive. Additionally, all organizations continually are experiencing increased costs associated with inventory. Because of these factors, firms are scrutinizing the way they manage inventories to ensure that the benefits of the functions of inventory justify their costs.

Inventory Functions

Inventories contribute to the overall organizational goals of good customer service and maximum operating efficiency. Without inventories, firms would not be able to operate effectively and efficiently. Only under the following ideal conditions would inventories not be needed:

1. Market demand is known with certainty.
2. Raw material procurement is instantaneous.
3. Work-in-process conversions are instantaneous.
4. Finished goods production and distribution are instantaneous.
5. Production interruptions, such as equipment maintenance, strikes, and so on, never occur.
6. Quantity discounts on unit costs are not available.
7. Procurement (ordering and/or setup) costs are insignificant.

It is because these conditions are rarely found that inventories exist in virtually all organizations.

Inventories do provide functional benefits to firms. The primary function of inventories is to act as a suspension system does in an automobile. Inventories buffer the organization when there are differences between market demand and production/sales capabilities. Changes in market demands can be absorbed by inventory, just as the automobile suspension system absorbs differences in the levels of the road surfaces. Inventories may be classified functionally according to the shocks or conditions they are designed to absorb.

1. Smoothing inventories — inventory for an industrial, retail, wholesale, or financial institution carried to decouple sales or usage from receipts including: finished or semi-finished goods carried to decouple production from seasonal market demand for a manufacturer; work-in-process to decouple production processes and departments; raw materials carried to decouple production from suppliers; and supplies carried to decouple usage from receipts.

2. Transit (pipeline) inventories—inventories in transit between supplier and producer; between processes within the production system; and between manufacturer, retailer, wholesaler, or financial institutions and the customer.

3. Precautionary inventories—inventories carried to buffer the company from uncertainties in: market demand; processing requirements and times; equipment breakdowns; labor absenteeism and efficiency; production yields and scrap rates; strikes; price increases; and record inaccuracy and management mistakes.

4. Lot size inventories—inventories carried to take advantage of procurement (ordering/setup) cost savings or of quantity discounts.

Inventory Costs

While inventories provide beneficial functions to the firm in terms of customer service and operating efficiencies, they also incur costs. Because resources are limited, most firms seek to minimize the investment in inventories. Thus, managing inventories revolves around balancing the costs and savings associated with or relevant to inventory levels. Relevant costs are those that vary with the level of inventory. Whether a cost is relevant or not may depend upon the situation. For example, the cost of an inventory item is relevant if it changes because of the amount ordered (i.e., a quantity discount). Relevant costs include variable out-of-pocket costs and the opportunity costs of forgone revenues, cost savings, or profits. Effective inventory management is based on minimizing the relevant or variable out-of-pocket and opportunity costs directly affected by the inventory decisions of how much and when to order.[1]

Variable Out-of-Pocket Costs

These are the costs which change in periodic total amount with changes in activities such as ordering, storing, and issuing inventory items. For example, variable restocking cost generally includes the costs of purchase order forms, receiving forms, and postage because the usage of these items tends to vary directly with the number of orders placed each period. Excluded from variable costs are all costs that do not change in periodic total amount when changes in activity occur. Depreciation on equipment used by the purchasing department is thus excluded when the activity change in question does not change the equipment in use. The question of variability and relevance, however, is a relative one. Although the personnel costs within a purchasing department are not affected by a decision to order one particular item 12 times a year instead of six, they will usually be affected by an inventory policy change that doubles the total number of orders placed in the department. These costs are usually semifixed costs and are not normally considered relevant to the inventory decision.

Opportunity Costs

Opportunity costs are the revenues or savings from alternative uses of assets that must be forgone when these assets are used for a specific purpose. Capital invested in inventory has an opportunity cost that is measured by what the same capital could earn in the best alternative use. One of the major components of inventory cost is the opportunity cost of capital tied up in the inventory. Similarly, the income forgone from alternative use of space utilized to store inventory may be considered an opportunity cost.

The following kinds of costs must be balanced in managing inventories.

1. *Procurement (ordering/setup) costs.* Includes those costs either of placing purchase orders with vendors for materials or those related to ordering a manufacturing lot from the plant. When material is purchased, costs are incurred for writing material requisitions and purchase orders, processing invoices, receiving and inspecting shipments, and delivering shipments to storage. When manufactured lots are produced, costs are incurred for paperwork activities, machine setups, initial production scrap, or defects.

2. *Carrying costs.* The costs incurred because of the volume or amount of inventory in stock. These costs are usually a function (percentage) of the dollar cost of the inventory. Carrying costs usually include:

   a. *Cost of capital invested.* Money invested in inventory is usually a major, if not the major, cost component.

It is the higher of either the marginal return on investment of the firm or the weighted average cost of capital. Unless the extra profit (or the reduced expense)
resulting from higher inventories is at least sufficient
to pay for the cost of capital incurred by the company,
the added inventory investment is not worthwhile.

b. *Costs of deterioration, damage, spoilage, and obsolescence.* These costs are incurred when inventory is no
longer salable because of physical deterioration,
damage, spoilage, or obsolescence due to changing
sales patterns or customer demand.

c. *Costs of storage.* Storing inventory incurs costs related to storeroom space, supervisory and operating
personnel, material handling equipment, and record-
keeping. These costs are often related to the size of
the item stored; however, most firms express the
costs as a percentage of the item stored.

d. *Insurance.* Inventories are assets that are usually
covered by company insurance policies. The costs are
the premiums for the policies and are directly related
to the value of the inventory.

e. *Taxes.* Many states have inventory taxes. The tax
cost of the inventory depends on the value of the
inventory being assessed at a tax rate (percentage).
The value may be determined at a point in time or as
an average over time, depending upon the tax law.

3. *Stockout costs.* The costs of not having inventory available when it is needed to satisfy a customer delivery date
or to meet a production schedule need. When finished
goods are not available to deliver to a customer, sales are
lost or back order costs are incurred. If sales are lost, the
stockout costs equal the forgone profit or contribution
margin plus a loss in goodwill (future sales). If the stockout is back ordered, costs are incurred to prepare and process related paperwork and possibly to pay high freight
premiums When materials needed for production are not in
stock, machine downtime and schedule interruption costs
may be incurred.

The procurement, deterioration, storage, insurance, taxes, and
backorder costs are variable out-of-pocket costs. The capital and lost
sales costs are opportunity costs. Procurement and stockout costs

are usually estimated at some value per order (or setup) or stockout occurrence. Carrying costs are usually estimated as a percentage of the value of the inventory.

Difficult problems arise in estimating the costs of inventories. Lost sales and other intangible costs are difficult to estimate. In addition, many of the costs of inventories are not readily available from the typical accounting system. As a result, estimates of inventory costs are frequently made with little reference to accounting records.

The cost concepts needed for inventory decision making differ markedly from the cost concepts employed by the accountant in measuring periodic profits. For example, the accountant accumulates costs by functions such as purchasing and stockkeeping. The costs recorded are the amount of cost incurred for the activity. Moreover, only those costs and revenues that at some time involve cash outlays and cash receipts are recorded in the accounts.

On the other hand, inventory costs are those future economic costs that may be expected to vary with inventory levels and orders. These costs include tangible out-of-pocket as well as intangible opportunity costs. Historical accounting data may be helpful in estimating the tangible out-of-pocket costs; however, analysis and reclassification are usually required because the cost classifications needed are not the same as those employed for determining periodic income. Accounting, sales, and production and financial data can be used to estimate the intangible costs. Records of sales orders received but not filled can be kept and the profit contributions lost can be computed even if estimating the cost of customer dissatisfaction is highly subjective. Similarly, company return on investment (ROI) objectives may be used to calculate aggregate or total inventory levels and determine implicit costs of capital for carrying inventory. These economic costs are difficult to measure precisely and are often implied by strategic decisions and policies that govern maximum and minimum levels of inventories.

Example

One manager surveyed stated that he really did not know how much inventory cost. Carrying costs were guesses at moving targets such as increases in insurance premiums and fluctuations in the cost of capital. Stockout costs were even less precise and extremely sensitive to the industry's competitive environment. But even more difficult to estimate than carrying or stockout costs were the costs of poor quality and production interruptions hidden by inventory. His company felt these costs were large but had difficulty putting numbers on them.

How Much to Order

The order size for purchased materials or produced items directly affects the inventory level and the costs of inventories. Large order sizes result in higher average levels of inventory and fewer orders being placed. Thus, large order sizes result in high carrying costs, low procurement costs, and low stockout costs.

There are two basic approaches to answering the "How much to order/produce?" question. They are:

1. *Fixed quantity, variable period approach.* Under this approach, as illustrated in Exhibit 2-1, the order size is a fixed quantity that is placed at variable times. Inventory is monitored continuously and when the on-hand inventory falls to a reorder point, then a fixed quantity is ordered. The well-known Economic Order Quantity and Economic Lot Size model (to be presented later) are examples of this approach.

2. *Variable quantity, fixed period approach.* Under this approach, as illustrated in Exhibit 2-2, the order size is a variable quantity that is placed at fixed periods. Inventory is reviewed periodically and orders are placed to bring the inventory up to some predetermined level.

Exhibit 2-1
Fixed Quantity, Variable Period Inventory Model

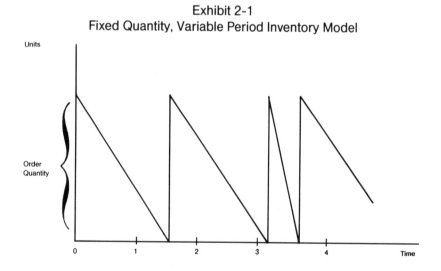

Exhibit 2-2
Variable Quantity, Fixed Period Inventory Model

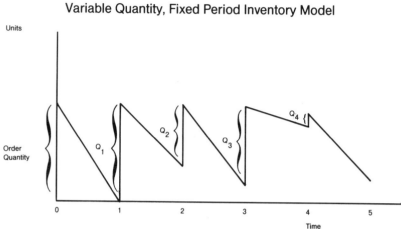

While the two approaches are mutually exclusive, it is possible to use one approach with one group of inventories and the other approach with other groups or classes of inventories. Thus, the manager should try to match the appropriate inventory model with particular inventory groups or classes of items.

Comparison of the Two Approaches

There are, of course, no hard and fast rules as to when one approach is better than the other. However, the following general observations apply.

In general, the *fixed order* approach is best for situations where items are ordered infrequently in large quantities compared to usage. Two-bin variations may be used for loose control of low-value items as, for example, in open-floor stocks of screws and bolts. Perpetual record systems may be used where closer monitoring and control of stock levels is desirable.

In general, the *fixed period* approach is best suited for situations where groups of items are ordered for replenishment relatively frequently from one source and/or joint shipping considerations are important. Some variations of this approach are used for tight control (i.e., through periodic physical check) of high-value items. This approach is generally less suited to those situations where the cost of ordering and high item value suggest infrequent large orders.

There is a systemic difference in the data processing requirements of the two approaches. The fixed quantity system requires constant monitoring and, as a result, requires greater data processing capabilities than the fixed period approach. Exhibit 2-3 is a summary of the major differences between the two approaches.

Exhibit 2-3
Comparison of the Two Approaches

Fixed Period, Variable Quantity	Fixed Quantity, Variable Period
1. Higher safety stock.	1. Lower safety stock.
2. Higher order costs.	2. Lower order costs.
3. Lower order quantities.	3. Higher order quantities.
4. Higher inventory.	4. Lower inventory.
5. Tracks demand.	5. Amplifies demand.
6. Lower data processing costs.	6. Higher data processing costs.

The question in inventory management is not to try to determine that one approach is better than the other but instead to try to determine which approach is better for a particular firm in a particular situation. In the following sections, the more widely used models for these approaches are presented.

Example

A small retailer had managed inventory by periodically reviewing the inventory in various departments. On Wednesdays, the inventory in housewares was reviewed and an order was placed for all houseware items needing replenishment. After the retailer was bought out by a retail chain store, point of purchase cash registers were installed that perpetually updated inventory records every time a sale was made. When the on-hand level reached a certain point, a centralized purchasing information system generated orders to replenish each retail store.

Fixed Quantity Model

Model 1 - Basic Economic Order Quantity

The economic order quantity is defined as that order quantity which best balances the inventory procurement costs against the inventory carrying costs. When these costs have been balanced, the total inventory costs are minimized. These relationships are illustrated in Exhibit 2-4.

Exhibit 2-4
Inventory Costs as a Function of Order Size

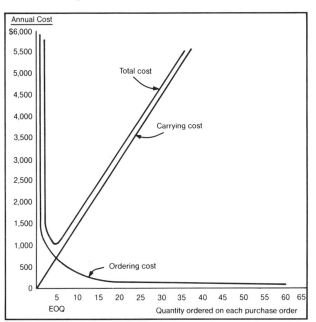

The EOQ concept applies only under the following conditions:

1. The demand and ordering lead time for the item is known and constant.

2. Orders are received in lots or batches equal to the order quantity.

If we further assume that there are no quantity discounts and stockouts are not allowed, we can quantitatively model the inventory cost function as follows:

(Equation 2.1)

$$TIC = (D/Q)S + (Q/2)CI$$

Where:

TIC = Total Inventory Cost
D = Annual Demand
S = Procurement Costs per Order
C = Item Cost
I = Carrying Cost Expressed as a Percentage of Item Cost
Q = Order Quantity

The EOQ is the order quantity Q that minimizes this cost function. The EOQ model may be illustrated with the following problem. Assume one wishes to determine how much to order of an item costing $720 with an annual demand of 60 units, a 30% carrying cost, and a procurement cost of $50 per order. The EOQ level can be derived either through trial and error or with a simple formula.

A *trial and error* approach is where different values of Q are used in Equation 2.1 until the minimum value is found. To illustrate, suppose monthly and annual demand are used as two extreme order quantities.

Exhibit 2-5
Inventory Levels of Alternative Inventory Policies

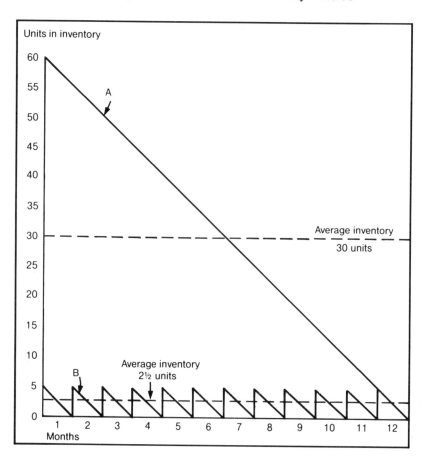

The resulting inventory levels of these two alternatives are shown in Exhibit 2-5. Line A represents the inventory on hand if the company decides to order 60 units at a time. If the company uses 60 units of this item in a year and if each item costs $720, a policy of ordering once a year implies that, on the date the shipment arrives, the company will have these 60 units on hand.[2] As units are sold or used, the quantity on hand declines until it reaches zero at the end of the year. At that time a new shipment is received. Because inventory falls from 60 units to zero units during the course of the year, the average inventory on hand, assuming the usage rate is fairly constant, is about 30 units. Line B represents the inventory on hand if the company orders five units at a time or one months' demand each time. As items are sold, the quantity on hand declines to zero at the end of the month. The average inventory on hand will be two and a half units. The relevant costs for the two inventory policies are summarized in Exhibit 2-6.

Exhibit 2-6
Relevant Costs for Inventory Policies

Order quantity	5	60
Cost per unit	$ 720	$ 720
Inventory investment:		
Beginning of period	$3,600	$43,200
End of period	0	0
Average inventory	$1,800	$21,600
Number of orders	12	1
Annual costs:		
Carrying cost		
(30% of average investment)	$ 540	$ 6,480
Order cost		
($50 per order)	$ 600	$ 50
Total relevant costs	$1,140	$ 6,530

It is clear that the company will reduce total inventory costs by ordering five units each time. While the once-a-year policy does reduce order (setup) costs, it causes a much greater increase in carrying cost.

Are the five units to be purchased with each order the optimum or best solution? Perhaps the cost of ordering on a weekly basis or once every two months would entail an even greater reduction in the total inventory cost. A calculation of the relevant costs in the manner illustrated in Exhibit 2-7 will show whether these policies would result in higher or lower costs than the cost of purchasing five units with each order.

Exhibit 2-7
Illustration of Total Cost Changes

Order quantity	3	4	5	10	60
Cost per unit	$ 720	$ 720	$ 720	$ 720	$ 720
Inventory investment:					
Beginning of period	$2,160	$2,880	$3,600	$7,200	$43,200
End of period	0	0	0	0	0
Average inventory	$1,080	$1,440	$1,800	$3,600	$21,600
Annual costs:					
Carrying cost (30% of average investment)	$ 324	$ 432	$ 540	$1,080	$ 6,480
Order cost ($50 per order)	$1,000	$ 750	$ 600	$ 300	$ 50
Total relevant costs	$1,324	$1,182	$1,140	$1,380	$ 6,530

In this particular case, it so happens that a policy of ordering five units each time is the optimum policy and any other policy would result in higher costs of ordering and carrying the inventory. These results are shown graphically in Exhibit 2-4. Notice that the total cost of purchases each year (60 units x $720) is not relevant because this cost will remain constant regardless of the number of orders placed (or the order quantity size).

For a company with many different items in inventory, the above discussion may be enlightening but it is not very useful. To determine the best order quantity by means of a trial and error calculation, the order clerk or production scheduler would have to compute the cost of several order size alternatives for each item in inventory. Clearly, this is a prohibitive task even assuming that many inventory items have similar characteristics so that the same table or graph may be used for several different stockkeeping items.

Fortunately, a simple formula is available for calculating the EOQ for a given item. Using the variables in Equation 2.1, the formula may be stated as:

$$EOQ = \sqrt{\frac{2DS}{CI}}$$ (Equation 2.2)

The formula is derived by setting the procurement costs equal to the carrying costs (from Equation 2.1) and solving for Q, the unknown.

Thus, for the previous problem the EOQ can be determined as follows:

$$EOQ = \sqrt{\frac{2DS}{CI}}$$
$$= \sqrt{\frac{(2)(60)(50)}{(720)(.30)}}$$
$$= \sqrt{27.28} \quad \text{or approximately five units.}$$

Note that this optimum or economic order quantity of five units is the same quantity as that suggested by the cost curve in Exhibit 2-4 and in the prior tabular presentation.

While the above equation was set up to express EOQ as the number of units to be purchased at a time, the equation can be set up to express EOQ in any of the following terms:

Terms in which EOQ is expressed	Variable D in EOQ formula	EOQ solution
Order quantity in units (as above)	60 units	5 units
Order quantity in monthly usage	12 units	one month's usage
Order quantity in dollars	$43,200	$3,600

These different solutions simply express the result in different forms. In order to obtain the desired answer in these various scales, the data to be inserted into the EOQ equation must be in corresponding terms.

A company should choose the equation that meets its own needs and available data. For example, if orders will be prepared from bin cards expressed in physical units, then perhaps EOQ and usage should be expressed in physical units. If, in contrast, the available data come from the perpetual inventory records expressed in dollars of cost, the company may find an expression using dollars more helpful.

Simplification of EOQ Formula

The basic EOQ formula can be simplified where some of the factors in the EOQ formula are constant for families of items carried in inventory. Suppose, for example, the cost of placing an order and carrying costs expressed as a percentage, is the same for all items in the inventory. Equation 2.2 can be simplified as follows, where K is a constant number for all items or groups of items in inventory.

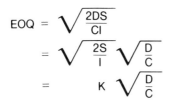

$$EOQ = \sqrt{\frac{2DS}{CI}}$$
$$= \sqrt{\frac{2S}{I}} \sqrt{\frac{D}{C}}$$
$$= K \sqrt{\frac{D}{C}} \qquad \text{(Equation 2.3)}$$

The original EOQ equation had four variables: annual usage (D), ordering cost (S), carrying cost per unit expressed as a percentage (I), and the cost of the item (C). Here, these four variables have been reduced to two. It is this equation that forms the basis for determining the combined costs of ordering and carrying that is implied by the existing order volumes and inventory levels. This simplified equation presents the two major variables that should influence the inventory policies of a company — annual usage and cost per unit.

As cost per unit increases, the firm should order more often and less items per order. The reverse is true if cost per unit declines. As the number of annual units sold or used increases, the EOQ should increase. The reverse is true for annual usage declines. It is annual usage and cost per unit that drive a reorder point system.

Changes in the EOQ because of changes in either annual usage or cost per unit or both are dampened by the square root function in the EOQ formula. Thus, effects on annual usage and cost per unit have less of an effect on EOQ. Therefore, minor errors or changes in either D or C may be ignored.

The EOQ formula does not consider fluctuations in usage for a particular inventory item. This type of inventory system does not track changes in demand very well because the annual, monthly, or other frequency of usage is estimated in advance, and there is no provision in the system for monitoring this estimate. Using the reorder-point system, it is possible to order an EOQ at the end of the season when future demand is expected to be small. Because the EOQ, once calculated, is usually reviewed infrequently, seasonality and other significant changes in usage are not reflected in a revised EOQ until such time as a review of the inventory ordering policies is made. In some systems this occurs on a very infrequent basis and sometimes only after the inventory has become obsolete or is so slow moving that attention is directed to it.

Few critical variables are estimated with certainty. The EOQ formula does not provide for probability analysis of the underlying variables or the determination of safety stock levels. The optimum level of safety stock is related to the "when to order" decision and will be discussed in Chapter 3. The EOQ formula uses one number for an invoice price (C); thus, any quantity discounts are ignored. However, there are techniques for considering quantity discounts.

Model 2 - EOQ with Quantity Discounts

The EOQ formula derived above does not take into consideration quantity discounts. Where quantity discounts are present, the inventory cost is a function of how many are ordered and may be expressed as:

$$TIC_j = \left(\frac{D}{Q_j}\right) S + \left(\frac{Q_j}{2}\right) C_j I + \left(C_j\right) D \qquad \text{(Equation 2.4)}$$

where j indicates price (cost) break points for various quantities. This cost function cannot be solved in a straightforward manner as is possible with Equation 2.1. However, there are approaches to deciding whether quantity discounts should be taken. The following example may be used to illustrate how this is done.

Assume the following data:
Order costs = \$24 per order
Carrying costs = 30% per year
Demand for an item = \$10,000 per year

$$EOQ = \sqrt{\frac{(2)(24)(10,000)}{.30}}$$

$$= \sqrt{1,600,000}$$

= \$1,265 or 7.9 orders per year or 1.5 months' supply.

Given that there is a 10% unit cost reduction on an order for $3,000, should the quantity discount be taken?

One might say a good buy is made when the reduction in unit cost is greater than the increased carrying cost incurred from purchasing the additional quantity. In this case, an average of 3.6 months' inventory would be carried at a cost of 2.5% per month instead of 1.5 months' inventory at a cost of 2.5% per month. This additional supply (3.6 minus 1.5) divided by two in order to get an average and then multiplied by 2.5% needs to be compared with the percentage reduction in unit cost. In this case the additional carrying cost is less than the 10% unit cost reduction so the additional supply should be purchased. This relationship can be expressed by the following equation:

$$100 \frac{(C_1 - C_2)}{C_1} \quad > \quad \frac{(N_2 - N_1)}{2} \qquad \text{(Equation 2.5)}$$

Where:

C_1 = unit cost without discount
C_2 = unit cost with discount
N_1 = number of months' supply without discount
N_2 = number of months' supply with discount
I = monthly carrying cost

Using the data from the example above:

$$100 \, (.10) \quad > \quad 2.5 \left(\frac{(3.6 - 1.5)}{2} \right)$$

$$10 \quad > \quad 2.6.$$

Thus, the discount should be taken.

Model 3 - Economic Lot Size (ELS) with Noninstantaneous Receipts

Frequently, an order or lot size is not delivered or received into stock all at once. This is usually the situation where manufacturing orders are produced and delivered into stock. While units are being produced, partial deliveries to stock are made at some production rate. However, withdrawals are also being made at some demand or usage rate so that the maximum inventory level does not equal the lot size as with the basic EOQ model.

Suppose a manufacturer sells 4,000 units a year of an item it manufactures. If it were to devote the facilities to that item exclusively, it could produce 24,000 units a year although the maximum sales are still 4,000 units. Thus, it takes only two months to turn out 4,000 units at full-capacity production. The manufacturer wants to know whether it would be better to devote the facilities exclusively to that item once a year for a two-month span of time (Alternative B) or to schedule production five times a year, with the two-month production period broken into five smaller segments of time (Alternative A).[3]

	Alternative A	Alternative B
Number of production runs	5	1
Total production (demand per year)	4,000 units	4,000 units
Production per production run	800 units	4,000 units
Total days of available production	360 days	360 days
Days per production run	12 days	60 days

The relevant costs for this decision, also assumed, are as follows:

Carrying cost of an item	—	30% of the production cost
Production cost per item	—	$6
Setup cost per production run	—	$120

Exhibit 2.8 shows the inventory levels of the alternative lot sizes. Notice that the maximum inventory is not equal to the lot size. Instead, it is equal to the rate of inventory buildup, which is the difference in production rate (P) and the demand rate (D), multiplied by the length of time that the buildup occurs, which is the lot size (Q) divided by the production rate (P). Thus, the maximum average inventories may be calculated with the following equations:

$$\text{IMAX} = (P - D)\frac{Q}{P} = \frac{(P - D)}{P}Q \qquad \text{(Equation 2.6)}$$

$$\text{IAVER} = \frac{\text{IMAX} + \text{IMIN}}{2} = \frac{\left(\frac{(P - D)}{P}\right)Q + 0}{2}$$

$$= \left(\frac{(P - D)}{P}\right)\frac{Q}{2} \qquad \text{(Equation 2.7)}$$

Exhibit 2-8
Economic Lot Size Inventory Levels for Alternatives A and B

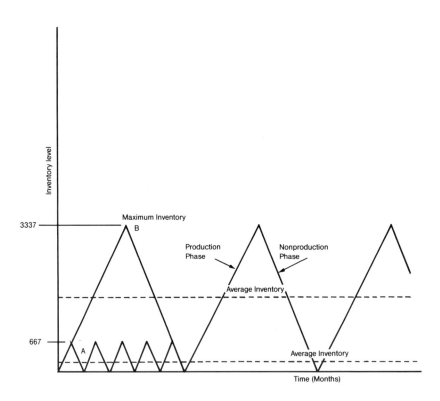

As shown in Exhibit 2-9, Alternative A is less costly. What about other possibilities? Might there be some other production policy that would result in still lower relevant costs? Once again, an algebraic solution is possible for determination of the Economic Lot Size (ELS). The total cost function shown below is similar to the basic EOQ cost function. The major difference is the correction factor $\sqrt{\dfrac{P}{P-D}}$ for determining average inventory.

$$TIC_{ELS} = (D/Q)S + \left(\frac{P-D}{P}\right)\left(\frac{Q}{2}\right)CI \qquad \text{(Equation 2.8)}$$

Exhibit 2-9
Costs Affected by Production Policy

	Production Policy	
	Alternative A	Alternative B
Quantity produced on each run	800 units	4,000 units
Inventory investment:		
Maximum inventory (quantity)	667 units	3,333 units
Minimum inventory (quantity)	0 units	0 units
Average inventory (quantity)	333 units	1,667 units
Average inventory (cost)	$2,000	$10,000
Annual costs:		
Carrying costs	$ 600	$ 3,000
Setup costs	600	120
Total relevant costs	$1,200	$ 3,120

Solving this equation to find the minimum total cost ELS results in the following formula for calculating ELS.

$$\text{ELS} = \sqrt{[(2DS)/CI)] \, [(P/(P - D)]} \qquad \text{(Equation 2.9)}$$

Where:

ELS = Economic Lot Size
D = Annual usage of a product
P = Maximum possible annual production of a product
C = Standard or estimated production cost per unit
S = Setup costs
I = Carrying cost expressed as a percentage of unit production cost

To illustrate use of this equation, consider the data used in the previous table. The Economic Lot Size may be determined as follows:

$$\text{ELS} = \sqrt{\frac{(2)(4,000)(120)}{(6)(.30)} \times \frac{(24,000)}{(24,000 - 4,000)}}$$

$$= \sqrt{\frac{960,000}{1.8} \times 1.2}$$

$$= \quad 800 \text{ units per production run.}$$

Apparently, the optimum policy is to produce five times a year with each production run being for 800 units. As seen in Exhibit 2-9, the total relevant costs for this lot size are $1,200, and any other policy will result in a higher total of carrying and setup charges.

Comparison of EOQ and ELS

There is a close relationship between the equation for the Economic Order Quantity (Equation 2.2) and the equation for the Economic Lot Size (Equation 2.8). For comparison, the two equations are presented as follows:

$$\text{EOQ} = \sqrt{2DS/(CI)} \qquad \text{ELS} = \sqrt{((2DS/(CI)) \times (P/(P-D))}$$

The two equations differ by the factor $\sqrt{P/(P-D)}$. It is assumed that the production rate (P) is greater than the usage rate (D); otherwise, the economic lot size is the production rate and inventory would not be built. Because P is usually greater than D, the factor $P/(P-D)$ will be greater than one, and the Economic Lot Size will be greater than the Economic Order Quantity for comparable cost and usage figures. In addition, the total inventory costs will be less because fewer lot sizes will be ordered and average inventory will simultaneously be lower.

The ELS model is also applicable for purchased items if delivery of the order size is provided at some noninstantaneous rate.

Example

A manufacturer of consumer products scheduled production each day in a rather unusual manner. Each morning, the plant manager would walk through the plant and shortly thereafter schedule production based on anticipated needs. Needless to say, the company was experiencing some degree of difficulty in managing inventories.

Other Economic Order Lot Models

Other models similar to the three presented above have been developed to calculate the economic order quantity under various circumstances. Quantitative order quantity models have been developed to incorporate uncertainty in demand, stockouts, families of items, warehouse capacity constraints, setup constraints, capital constraints, and other conditions. A review of these models is beyond the scope of this report but may be found in Brown[4] and Hadley and Whitin.[5]

Sensitivity Analysis

Estimates of the costs of carrying inventory and the ordering or setup costs are very difficult to calculate. To what extent can the results of the mathematical analysis outlined above be relied upon when the cost figures are lacking in precision? EOQ

As already suggested, when the economic order quantities are computed from imprecise cost estimates, the errors are dampened or muted by the presence of the square root function. Let us assume an extreme error in the estimate of ordering cost and compute the effect of this error on the economic order quantity and the total cost of ordering and carrying the inventory. The same principles and effects also apply to the economic lot size so only the economic order quantity will be illustrated.

The quantity to order, using the correct ordering cost of $50 is five units, computed as follows:

$$\text{EOQ} = \sqrt{\frac{2DS}{CI}} = \sqrt{\frac{(2)(60)(50)}{(.30)(720)}} = \sqrt{27.28} = 5 \text{ units}$$

Using an incorrect ordering cost of $200, four times the correct amount, the economic order quantity is:

$$\text{EOQ} = \sqrt{\frac{(2)(60)(200)}{(.30)(720)}} = \sqrt{111} = 10 \text{ units}$$

Note that an estimate of ordering cost that is four times as high as it should be results in a figure for economic order quantity that is only twice as high as it should be. The square root function has diminished the effect of the excessive estimate of order cost. Other errors would be diminished equally.

A 100% error is, of course, serious but just how great is the effect of this error on the total costs of ordering and carrying inventory? If the order quantity is 10 units, then the average inventory on hand from one order to the next will be approximately five units. Given per unit costs of $720, the average investment in inventory is, therefore, five times $720 or $3,600, and the carrying cost is 30% of $3,600 or $1,080. For the annual consumption of 60 units, an ordering policy of ordering 10 at each time will require six purchase orders rather than 12. Because each purchase order (and the other related costs of replenishing) equals $50, ordering costs will be $300. The total relevant costs for this ordering policy, as compared with the relevant costs for the correct policy of purchasing five units at a time, follow:

EOQ	5 units	10 units	Change in % 100%
Carrying cost	$ 540	$1,080	100%
Ordering cost	600	300	-50%
Total cost	$1,140	$1,380	21%

Carrying cost has increased as the result of buying too many units at a time, but this increase has been partly offset by the reduction in ordering cost. Total relevant cost has increased by only 21% in spite of the 100% increase in ordering quantity. In summary, a 400% error in the estimate of ordering cost has caused a 100% error in the quantity ordered which in turn caused a 21% error in the cost of ordering and carrying inventory. An extreme error in the estimate of ordering cost has been chosen to illustrate that in inventory management a bull's eye is not necessary. A near miss will do.

Similar errors in the estimate of the carrying cost (I) will have a similar effect on the estimated economic order quantity. What of the effect of errors in the estimates of both the ordering cost and the carrying cost? Because ordering cost appears in the numerator and carrying cost in the denominator, errors that occur in the same direction will tend to cancel each other out. If ordering cost and carrying cost are both in error by the same percentage and in the same direction, the resulting figures for economic order quantity will not be affected. If the errors are in opposite directions, this would accentuate the error in the estimate of economic order quantity. An error in the order quantity will cause either order costs or carrying costs to increase, but not both. An order quantity that is too high results in a greater carrying cost for inventory, which is partly offset by a lower ordering cost. An order quantity that is too low results in a higher than optimum ordering cost, but it is partly offset by the lower carrying cost.

Example

Companies have a difficult time establishing the carrying cost percentage and/or order costs. One company used a sensitivity analysis and found that within certain ranges, the EOQ values did not materially change. Because they believed the carrying cost and order cost would fall within this range, they were able to use any of the values within the range without materially distorting the results. This provided additional creditability to the use of the EOQ formula.

While the EOQ models are relatively insensitive to imprecision in estimates of the parameters used in the formulas, the models are not insensitive to deviations from the underlying assumptions. One of the more serious problems with using the reorder-point models occurs when demand is not constant. Periodic review and time-phased ordering models perform better when demand is not constant over time.

Periodic Review Models

Periodic review or fixed period approaches are time-based inventory management approaches. There are two parameters that must be selected for a periodic review approach. They are the fixed interval of time for review of the inventory position and the maximum inventory level from which all order quantities are calculated. The size of the order is the difference between this maximum predetermined level and the on-hand inventory position. (When the fixed order period is shorter than the order lead time period, the inventory position equals the on-order and on-hand inventory.)

The fixed interval of time for review of the inventory position may be daily, weekly, monthly, or some other period as established by management. Usually costs are not considered in establishing this time frame, but, instead, other factors such as the following may influence the review policy:

1. Desire to level the workload of the purchasing department.
2. Shelf life of the product.
3. Possible technological advances in the product.

4. Potential changes in style.
5. Seasonal patterns of demand which may change from year to year — i.e., demand for heating oil is dependent upon different weather conditions each year.
6. Frequent discounted prices of merchandise where each discounted price may involve different groups of items.
7. Frequent changes in sales mix.
8. Custom ordering or manufacturing of products with special requirements.

Other factors, of course, may be added to this list. The listing is not intended to be all inclusive but merely to demonstrate that there are situations where the required order quantity should be changed each time an order is placed. In that type of environment, a fixed period, variable quantity approach may be best.

The basic equations for all periodic review models are:

$$M = D(L + R) + S$$

and

$$Q = M - OH \qquad \text{(Equation 2.10)}$$

Where:

M   = predetermined maximum level of inventory,
D   = expected demand,
L   = order lead time,
R   = review time period,
S   = safety stock,
Q   = order quantity, and
OH = on-hand inventory.

The value of S is dependent upon:
1. the uncertainty of demand (D),
2. the uncertainty in the lead time (L),
3. fluctuations in demand levels,
4. standard quantities for shipping,
5. available warehouse space,
6. the value of the inventory item, and
7. the desired service level.

Numerous quantitative models have been developed to reflect different assumptions about these factors. Highly mathematical models have been formulated to find the optimal value of S (and, thereby, M and Q) when all costs are known and all other variables are specified. At the other extreme, the level of S (and, thereby, Q and M) may be determined based on experience and intuition.

An intermediate approach is to set a customer service level policy based on management judgment and then determine S by using this service level as a probability of meeting customer demand. Rarely are the costs of stockouts known with sufficient precision to find the optimal value of S. However, most organizations are able to develop a customer service policy reflecting the appropriate probability of meeting customer demand given the organizational strategy.

The value of S is based on the variability of demand over the lead time and the review period and the desired probability of meeting that demand. The safety stock (S) must protect the inventory level over the lead time (L) and the order period interval (R) because once an order is placed at time period t, another order cannot be placed until time t + R, and the second order will not be received until the lead time elapses at time t + R + L.

There are several ways to define service levels and each results in a different value of S. The three most commonly used service level definitions are:

1. percent of service per order cycle (interval),
2. percent of service per year, and
3. fraction of units demanded.

The selection of the service level definition by management implies a cost of service failure. The solution to the order size question for the various periodic review models can be illustrated with the following problem.

The monthly demand for an item is normally distributed with a mean of 200 units and a standard deviation of 20. Orders are placed every two months and arrive one month after they have been placed. The service level is 90% per order interval or 10% stockout probability during the order interval.

The service level fraction per interval equals one minus the fraction of stockouts per order interval or:

Service level (SL) = 1 - P (D(L + R)) M)   (Equation 2.11)
                   = 1 - P(Stockout fraction
                          per order interval)   (Equation 2.12)

For this service level definition, the formula to calculate M is:

$$M = D(L + R) + Z(SD) \sqrt{L + R}$$ (Equation 2.13)

Where: Z = the value related to level of desired customer service and may be found in any basic statistical text, and
        SD = a standard deviation derived from the demand for the inventory item.

For the problem just illustrated, P(stockout fraction) = .10 and the Z value for 90% is 1.28 (taken from a normal or Z table).

$$M = 200(1 + 2) + 1.28(20) \sqrt{3}$$
$$= 644 \text{ units.}$$

The following table shows how the service level and safety stock are related for the sample problem.

Service Level	Safety Stock	M
.80	29	629
.90	44	644
.95	57	657
.98	71	671

Increasingly greater amounts of safety stock are needed to increase the service level. While the above results relate to the problem just illustrated, similar conclusions hold for other types of periodic review models and definitions of service levels. Formulas exist to calculate the values of S and M for other periodic review systems.

Time-Phased Ordering Models

Time-phased ordering models are a special case of the fixed period, variable quantity approach. These models are used most frequently in conjunction with dependent demand items in material requirements planning systems. Because these models simultaneously address the questions of how much and when to order in dependent demand environments, treatment of these models is presented in Chapter 4.

Survey Results

Based upon the survey results, firms use experience more frequently than quantitative models or formulas in setting order quantities. This is not surprising as one would expect all managers to use experience and judgment even when quantitative models are employed. What is surprising about the results shown in Exhibit 2-10 is the relatively infrequent use of such quantitative models. Quantitative models are found most frequently in setting order quantities for raw materials (39.1%) and finished goods (37.8%). Work-in-process, supplies, and service parts appear to be ordered on an as-needed basis for a large number of firms.

Exhibit 2-10
Survey Frequency of Use of Quantitative Models and Experience
in Setting Order Quantities

	Method for Setting Order Quantities	
	Quantitative Models	Experience
Manufacturing Respondents		
Raw Materials	39.1%	63.0%
Work-in-Process	30.4	26.7
Finished Goods (and		
Merchandise)	37.8	71.1
Supplies	8.9	65.2
Service Parts	11.1	60.9
Nonmanufacturing Respondents		
Merchandise (and		
Finished Goods)	41.6	87.5
Supplies	12.5	29.2

The time-phased ordering approaches, MRP and DRP, are the most frequently used inventory management systems for deciding how much (and when) to order. As shown in Exhibit 2-11, the fixed order quantity system is the next most frequently used system, particularly for supplies and raw materials inventories in manufacturing firms and for retailing inventories in nonmanufacturing companies. Fixed time period systems are used overall by less than one out of 10 of the respondents.

Exhibit 2-11
Frequency of Use of Types of Inventory Management Systems

| | Type of System | | |
	Fixed Order Quantity System	Fixed Time Period System	MRP/ DRP
Manufacturing Respondents			
Raw Materials	27.3%	10.9%	69.1%
Work-in-Process	16.4	3.6	56.3
Finished Goods (and			
Merchandise)	21.9	10.9	72.7
Supplies	27.3	10.9	10.9
Service Parts	18.2	5.5	27.3
Nonmanufacturing Respondents			
Merchandise (and Finished			
Goods)	25.9	7.4	48.1
Supplies	11.1	3.7	-
Service Parts	-	-	7.4

Summary

    Inventories are a significant portion of many firms' assets and cost of goods sold. Because inventories are not self-correcting, they must be effectively managed to minimize the costs of inventories. These costs include variable out-of-pocket and opportunity costs that are not easily measured. Accounting data used to measure periodic profits may be of little value in managing inventories.

    Inventory management revolves around deciding how much to order and when to order. Various approaches and models are presented in this chapter to answer the "How much to order?" question.

    Survey results indicate that experience is used much more frequently than quantitative models to set order quantities. What is surprising is the relatively infrequent use of quantitative models to supplement experience-based decision making. A minority of firms seem to be relying strictly on quantitative models, while others rely strictly on experience or a combination of experience and models. The relatively infrequent use of quantitative models indicates that the advances in inventory theory over the past 30 years have been unevenly applied in industry.

Time-phased ordering approaches, including MRP and DRP, are the most frequently used inventory management systems. These systems are found in more than 72% of the manufacturing respondents and in more than 48% of the nonmanufacturing respondents. Fixed time period systems are used in approximately one out of 10 responding firms. Fixed order quantity systems are used to some extent but not nearly as much as the volume of inventory theory would support.

Notes

[1] Fixed costs are usually not relevant for inventory decisions. In most situations these fixed costs may be considered sunk costs.

[2] It is assumed that no safety stock is kept on hand. The presence or absence of safety stock would not change the analysis. We would still be trying to minimize the costs related to the cycle stock — i.e., the portion of inventory over and above the safety stock.

[3] For simplicity in making the calculations, it has been assumed that the year has 360 days. All calculations are in terms of calendar days rather than working days. To convert to working days, it would be necessary to deduct the holidays.

[4] Brown, R. G. *Statistical Forecasting for Inventory Control*, New York: McGraw-Hill Book Co., 1959.

[5] Hadley, G. and T. M. Whitin. *Analysis of Inventory Systems*, Englewood Cliffs, N. J.: Prentice-Hall, Inc., 1983.

Chapter 3

When to Order

Inventory management requires two decisions: how much to order and when. In much of the previous chapter, models were developed for different approaches to answering the "how much to order" question. These models are primarily concerned with balancing ordering/setup costs and carrying costs of inventories. In this chapter, models are presented that focus on answering the "when to order" question so that the carrying costs of safety stock are balanced with the stockout costs of not carrying a sufficient amount of safety stock.

Fixed Order Quantity Approach

For the fixed order quantity approach, the "when to order" problem is one of deciding how low inventory may fall before placing a replenishment order. Assume a company places an order whenever inventory falls to 30 units. If it waits until inventory on hand is 20 units, it would, on the average, have less inventory in stock and the cost of carrying inventory would be less. However, there may be a risk in waiting too long before placing an order and the company may run out of inventory before the replenishment arrives. This stockout may result in a loss of profit either because goods are not available for customers when they want to buy or because the lack of materials may hold up production.

Model 1 - Fixed Order Quantity (EOQ) Model

As discussed in Chapter 2, the fixed order quantity system continuously monitors the inventory level, and a replenishment order is placed when the inventory (on hand plus on order) reaches a reorder point (ROP). For the basic EOQ model, there is no uncertainty in demand or lead time and stockouts are not allowed. The "when to order" decision in this situation is shown in Exhibit 3-1.

Exhibit 3-1
When to Order Decision

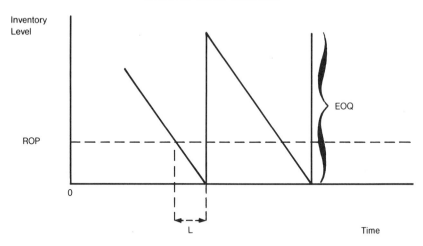

An order is placed when the inventory reaches a level equal to the demand during the lead time. The following equation is used to calculate the reorder point.

$$ROP = U_L - R \qquad \text{(Equation 3.1)}$$

Where:

ROP = reorder point

U_L = usage during lead time

R = items ordered but not yet received

Using the above formula, assume that a company issues 10 units a day from the stockroom, and the lead time for replenishment of the item is eight days. If there are no units on order, the ROP may be calculated as follows:

$$ROP = (10)(8) - 0$$
$$= 80 \text{ units}$$

In the above equation, the term R is always zero unless the EOQ is such that the amount received as an economic order quantity does *not* raise the level of inventory above the reorder point. In that situation, there are overlapping orders and the value of R is the number of units ordered but not yet received. Using the data from the above example with an order EOQ of 60 units, the reorder point is calculated as follows:

$$ROP = (10)(8) \quad - \quad (60)$$
$$= 20 \text{ units}$$

This is illustrated in Exhibit 3-2, where there are overlapping orders. The maximum inventory is 60 units and the minimum inventory zero. Remember that this type of situation only occurs where the EOQ or ELS does not increase the level of inventory to that amount used during lead time.

Exhibit 3-2
Example of Overlapping Orders and Reorder Point

Day	Beginning Balance	Received	Issued	On Order	Ending Balance
1	60		10	60	50
2	50		10	60	40
3	40		10	60	30
4	30		10	60	20
5	20		10	120	10
6	10	60	10	60	60
7	60		10	60	50
8	50		10	60	40
9	40		10	60	30
10	30		10	60	20
11	20		10	120	10
12	10	60	10	60	60
13	60		10	60	50
14	50		10	60	40
15	40		10	60	30
16	30		10	60	20
17	20		10	120	10
18	10	60	10	60	60

Model 2 - EOQ with Stockouts Allowed and Stockout Costs Known

Determining the optimal reorder point when stockouts are allowed and when stockout costs are known revolves around balancing safety stock carrying costs and stockout costs of backorders. Incurring backorders may be efficient, but lost sales would never occur since demand is known with certainty for the EOQ model.

Example

One inventory manager discovered that his initial backorder experience was much lower than might be expected from the newly installed system because his clerks were adept at "cheating" the system. While these order clerks followed the main elements of the system, they were often able to anticipate large customer orders before they arrived; they frequently engaged in expediting maneuvers, and sometimes simply neglected to enter backorder forms when they knew that a supplier's shipment would be received in the next day or two. The stockouts were there, and they took their toll on the company in terms of irritation, delay, and expediting expense; however, the brief stockouts never resulted in backorders and the company management had not been fully aware of their extent and existence.

Suppose a mail-order retailer is willing to accept an out-of-stock situation and decides not to place a replenishment order until inventory has fallen to one week's demand, or 50 units. In this case, after inventory is depleted, the firm will be out of stock for a week before the replenishment order arrives. As shown in part B of Exhibit 3-3, the quantity backordered will be 50 units by the time the replenishment order arrives.

Reduced carrying costs explain the retailer's motive in deliberately permitting this stockout condition. But stockouts also cost money. There may be a cost of preparing and following up on a backorder. There is also the hard-to-measure but very important cost of delaying a customer, including the potential loss of future sales. In other words, the retailer must make a decision in which two sets of opposing costs are balanced: the costs of carrying inventory and the cost of stockouts. Again, the retailer is attempting to derive an optimum or least-cost situation.

To illustrate this problem, assume that the cost of carrying inventory is 20% of the cost of the goods purchased and that each of the items costs $5. If a replenishment order of 200 units is placed two weeks before inventory will be exhausted, average inventory will be 100 units, average investment $500, and the cost of carrying inventory $100.

Exhibit 3-3
Influence of Stockouts on Reorder Point

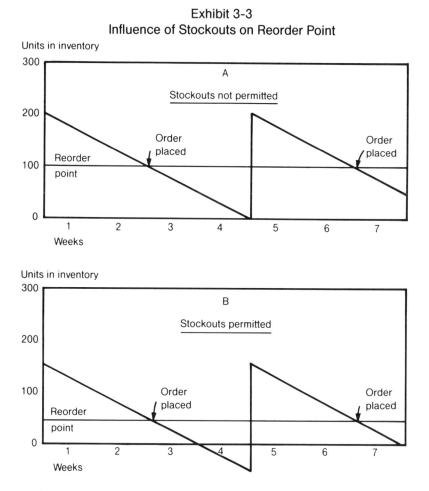

If a replenishment order is placed when inventory falls to 50 units, then the average inventory during the three weeks out of four that the retailer has inventory in stock is only 75 units; the average investment carried throughout the year is $281.25 (75% of 75 or 56.25 units at $5 per unit) and the 20% carrying cost is $56.25 per year. The retailer reduces the carrying cost from $100 to $56.25, saving $43.75, by waiting until inventory has fallen to 50 units before placing a replenishment order.

This decrease in carrying cost is partly offset by an increase in stockout, or shortage, cost. Suppose that stockout costs are proportional to the number of units and time out of stock. Also assume that the retailer, while he/she has no exact information about the cost in terms of customer dissatisfaction, feels that the cost of being out of stock is approximately six cents per week for each item out of stock, or about $3 per year. Because there will be an average of 25 units out of stock during the week immediately preceding receipt of the replenishment order, the cost of being out of stock during the week is $1.50. One week out of stock for each of the four-week periods amounts to a total of 13 out-of-stock weeks during the year. If each week out of stock costs the company $1.50, then the 13 weeks out of stock will cost $19.50. Summarizing and comparing costs of the two policies:

	Order when inventory falls to 100 units	Order when inventory falls to 50 units
Carrying cost	$100.00	$56.25
Stockout cost	0.00	19.50
Total relevant cost	$100.00	$75.75

The retailer will be better off to wait until inventory has fallen to 50 units before placing a reorder. However, this is not necessarily the best policy. Would it be better to reduce holding cost even further, or to reduce stockout costs by ordering when 75 units are in inventory? To answer questions like these, we need a more general solution than is possible with the above numerical examples. The optimum solution occurs when the inventory, immediately after a reorder is received (Z), bears the following relationship to these cost elements:

$$Z = \frac{(Q)\, C_2}{C_1 + C_2}$$

Where:

C_1 represents the carrying cost per unit of the item purchased (corresponding to CI in the previous chapter

C_2 represents the cost per year of being out of stock by one unit, and

Q represents the economic order quantity.

Consequently, the reorder point, ROP, is:

$$ROP = \frac{(Q)\, C_2}{C_1 + C_2} - U_L \qquad \text{(Equation 3.2)}$$

where U_L = usage during the lead time for replenishing inventory.

Applying this equation to the previous numerical illustration, where:

C_1 = (carrying cost) was $1 per item per year,
C_2 = (stockout penalty) was $3 per item per year,
Q was 200 units, equal to four weeks sales, so that,
U_L = 100 units during the two-week lead time, then
ROP = (200 (3/(1+3))) - 100
   = (200)(.75) - 100
   = 50 units.

Apparently, the policy depicted in Part B of Exhibit 3-3 is the optimum or best policy. If the company does not place a replenishing order until inventory has fallen to 50 units, the level of inventory immediately after receipt of a replenishment will be 150 units, the optimum quantity as indicated by the above computation.

Because the relationship $C_2 / (C_1 + C_2)$ is basic to an understanding of material in this chapter, it is worth exploring its implications. Given that C_1 is $1, then, for various stockout penalties, the optimum shelf inventory immediately following a replenishment is as follows:

Stockout penalty (C_2)	$\dfrac{C_2}{C_1 + C_2}$	Optimum inventory after replenishment
1	1/2	100
2	2/3	133
3	3/4	150
10	10/11	182
100	100/101	198
1000	1000/1001	200*

*Approximately.

In other words, the higher the stockout penalty, the smaller the number of units out of stock should be, and the greater, therefore, would be the optimum inventory immediately after an order is received. This relationship appeals directly to common sense. If the backorder system is inexpensive, and if customers are patient, there is little need to avoid stockouts. It is better to reduce carrying costs by lowering the overall level of inventory even at the cost of incurring some stockouts. Where the backorder system requires extensive paperwork and expediting procedures, and where disgruntled customers may take their business elsewhere, stockouts should be brief and back orders few.

Similarly, the optimum inventory after replenishment can, given a stockout penalty (say $3), be computed for various carrying costs:

Carrying cost (C_1)	$\dfrac{C_2}{C_1 + C_2}$	Optimum inventory after replenishment
1	3/4	150
2	3/5	120
3	3/6	100
10	3/13	46
100	3/103	6
1000	3/1003	0*

* Approximately.

The relationship also agrees with common sense. It pays to stock the items that cost little to carry, but it is better to incur stockout penalties than to stock those items whose carrying cost is very high.

The foregoing discussion of the stockout problem under conditions of certainty about future sales has been presented primarily to clarify the relationship between carrying costs and stockout penalties. It should not be applied to an actual situation without determining that the underlying assumptions are applicable. For example, a wholesaler placing orders for office supplies three times a year would not find the above analysis applicable without modification. The above analysis assumes that the rate of sales is constant (for example, 50 units per week) whereas the wholesaler may find that most of its supplies are sold at the beginning of a quarter. Similarly, a supermarket located close to a competitor should not apply this analysis without modification. It is not enough for the supermarket to increase stockout penalties to allow for loss of profit on individual items not sold. The above analysis assumes that sales are given and are not affected by stockouts; certainly a supermarket cannot presume that its sales will be unaffected by stockouts. Furthermore, the assumption that future sales are known with anything approximating certainty will seldom be appropriate.

For Models 1 and 2, there is no need for safety stock. The patterns of usage and lead time are uniform and known with certainty. We rarely find situations like this. The more likely situation is where usage and/or lead time are uncertain, and prudent inventory management provides for some level of safety stock to protect the company against stockouts. The reorder point and the average level of inventory are increased by the amount of safety stock as indicated by the relationships shown in Exhibit 3-4.

Exhibit 3-4
Reorder Point with Uncertain Demand and/or Lead Time

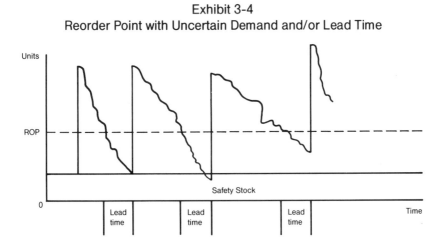

It is usually desirable to provide some degree of protection against stockouts due to these uncertainties. However, safety stock incurs carrying costs. The problem is to provide adequate protection. Equation 3.1 may be revised to incorporate safety stock as shown below:

$$ROP = U_L + Safety\ stock - R \qquad (Equation\ 3.3)$$

Management may use some average amount of safety stock to be carried at all times. Using the example above with an average safety stock of 20 units:

ROP = (10)(8) + 20 − 60
     = 40 units.

Safety stock levels based on constant amounts, average levels, or percentage of demand levels do not provide optimal policies because these rules do not attempt to balance safety stock stockout costs with carrying costs. The following models may be used to determine the optimal level of safety stock and, thereby, the optimal reorder point.

Model 3 - Variable Demand, Constant Lead Time - Known Backorder Stockout Costs Per Unit

While the demand for an item in the future is usually not known, it may be possible to approximate the probability distribution of such demand. The assumption of a constant lead time is frequently realistic, particularly when the variation in lead time is small in relation to the average lead time. With backorders, unsatisfied demand can be filled from a replenishment order, and the stockout costs include only the paperwork and disruption costs associated with each unit backordered.

The following equation relates the optimum probability of a stockout, $P(S)$, to a ratio of carrying costs to backorder costs.

$$P(S) = C_1(Q) / C_2(D)$$ (Equation 3.4)

Where:
   C_1 = carrying cost per unit of inventory per year,
   C_2 = backordering cost per unit,
   Q = order quantity, and
   D = annual expected demand.

If the probability distribution of demand is known, this equation can be used to determine the reorder point value that has the minimum carrying and stockout costs. The following examples may be used to illustrate this decision model.

Assume the following data:

D = 1,800/yr,
S = \$30 per order,
C_1 = \$.30 per unit per year, and
C_2 = \$1 per unit backordered.

Demand during lead time (D_{LT})	Probability $P(D_{LT})$	Probability of demand $\rangle$ D_{LT} or $P(S)$
20	.02	.98
21	.03	.95
22	.09	.86
23	.20	.66
24	.21	.45
25	.19	.26
26	.15	.11
27	.07	.04
28	.04	.00
	1.00	

To solve the problem, first calculate the EOQ and then find the probability of a stockout, P(S):

$$\text{EOQ} = \sqrt{(2\,(1800)\,(30))\,/\,.30} = 600 \text{ units}$$
$$\text{P(S)} = (.30)(600)\,/\,(1)(1{,}800) = .10.$$

As indicated in the last column of the demand during lead time distribution, the optimum P(S) = .10 is reordering when inventory is between 26 and 27. Therefore, the reorder point is 27 because its associated P(S) is the next probability to the optimum value of .10.

In similar fashion, suppose the demand during the lead time was normally distributed with a mean of 24 and a standard deviation of demand of 2 as shown in the graph on page 50.

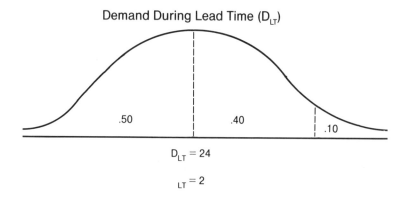

Demand During Lead Time (D_{LT})

.50   .40   .10

$D_{LT} = 24$

$_{LT} = 2$

The optimum P(S) is still .10. However, demand is distributed continuously. The Z value for .90 or 1 - P(S) is 1.256. Using the Z transformation equation:

$$Z_{(1 - P(S))} = \frac{ROP - D_{LT}}{\sigma\, LT} \qquad\qquad \text{(Equation 3.5)}$$

We can find the ROP as follows:

$$
\begin{aligned}
Z_{(1 - P(S))} &= Z_{90} &= 1.256 \\
D_{LT} &= 24 \\
_{LT} &= 2 \\
1.256 &= \frac{ROP - 24}{2} \\
ROP &= 26.51 \text{ or } 27 \text{ units.}
\end{aligned}
$$

The optimum reorder point is 27 units. Because the average demand during the lead time is 24 units, the optimal safety stock is three units.

This problem assumed the normal distribution to illustrate how to solve for the optimum ROP when demand is continuously distributed. However, equations and tables are available for other distributions such as the poisson and exponential. Additionally, models and equations are available for stockout costs related to lost sales and for stockout costs per outage or occurrence as well as costs per unit stockout.

Model 4: Variable Demand, Constant Lead Time — Unknown Stockout Costs

As indicated in Chapter 2, because stockout costs are not easily or precisely estimated, many organizations subjectively set a service level from which "optimal" reorder points can be determined. Such reorder points are established to meet specified service levels and are not derived from models minimizing explicit costs but instead imply the relative importance of carrying safety stock versus not carrying safety stock and incurring a stockout. Thus, they are optimal in the sense of being the best to meet the specified service level.

There are various definitions of the term service level. The service level used for the periodic review model discussed in Chapter 2 was the service per order interval. This service level definition indicates the probability of not running out of stock during an order interval and may be acceptable if the review period is the same for all products, which is frequently the case in fixed period approaches. However, where the order cycles differ among products, as in the fixed quantity models, the frequency of service per order cycle definition does not allow for uniform treatment of different products. Stockout frequencies of different items are not comparable when each item has different ordering cycles and different lead times. In these cases, a better definition of service level is the frequency of service per year.

The service level fraction per year (SL) is equal to one minus the stockout fraction per year, where the stockout fraction per year is equal to the number of annual order cycles (D/Q) multiplied by the stockout fraction per order cycle $(P(D_{LT} > ROP))$. The equations for this model are as follows:

$$SL = 1 - (D/Q) P(D_{LT} > ROP) \qquad \text{(Equation 3.6)}$$

or

$$P(D_{LT} > ROP) = Q/D (1 - SL) \qquad \text{(Equation 3.7)}$$

where

SL = the service level fraction per year,
D = annual expected demand,
D_{LT} = demand during the lead time,
Q = the economic order quantity, and
ROP = the reorder point.

Suppose a company has specified an 85% service level and thus has a 15% stockout level fraction per year. What should the order quantity and reorder point be if:

$$D = 18,000 \text{ units per year,}$$
$$S = \$400 \text{ per order, and}$$
$$CI = \$10 \text{ per unit per year.}$$

Demand during lead time D_{LT}	Probability $P(D_{LT})$	Probability of stockout $P(S)$
80	.025	.975
90	.100	.875
100	.200	.675
110	.350	.325
120	.200	.125
130	.100	.025
140	.025	0
	1.000	

The EOQ $= \sqrt{2(D)(S) / CI}$

$\qquad = \sqrt{2(18,000)(400) / 10}$

$\qquad = 1,200 \text{ units}$

and the stockout level fraction per order cycle is

$$P(D_{LT} > ROP) = (1,200/18,000)(1 - .85)$$
$$= .01$$

Referring to the $P(S)$ column above, the desired stockout level fraction per order cycle of .01 is between reorder points 130 and 140; therefore, the desired ROP is 140 units.

Reorder point calculations are simplified if demand is distributed according to some known distribution, such as the normal, poisson, or negative exponential. If the demand during the lead time in the above problem was distributed normally with a mean (D_{LT}) of 110 and a standard deviation (σ_{LT}) of 12 units, a service level stockout fraction per order cycle of .01 indicates the following ROP calculations. (The Z value for $Z_{(1-.01)}$ is 2.33. This may be found in a normal distribution or Z table included in almost all statistical books.)

$$ROP = D_{LT} + (Z_{SL}) + (\sigma_{LT}) \qquad \text{(Equation 3.8)}$$
$$ROP = 110 + 2.33(12)$$
$$= 138 \text{ units.}$$

Thus, 28 units of safety stock (138 - 110) are needed to ensure that the 85% service level fraction per year is achieved.

Exhibit 3-5 shows the impact of various service levels on annual stockouts and safety stock levels for this sample problem. As the service level fraction per year increases, the annual number of stockouts decreases linearly. However, the safety stock requirements to achieve these results increases in a nonlinear fashion. It takes increasingly greater levels of safety stock to increase the service level. A company can use these relationships to estimate the relative costs of stockouts as compared with the carrying costs of safety stocks; that is, for a desired service level of .90 the estimated cost of .75 (2.25 - 1.50) stockouts is greater than the carrying cost of one (29 - 28) additional unit of safety stock. For a desired service level of .98, the estimated cost of .45 (.75 - .30) stockouts is greater than the carrying costs of four (37 - 33) additional units of safety stock. Without knowing the exact costs of stockouts, firms can develop tradeoff charts in order to select optimal service levels.

Exhibit 3-5

Illustration of Table Used to Compute Tradeoffs

Service Level Fraction Per Year (SL)	Stockout Level Fraction Per Cycle $P(D_{LT} > ROP)$[1]	Annual Stockouts [2]	Safety Stock [3]
.80	.013	3.00	27
.85	.010	2.25	28
.90	.007	1.50	29
.95	.003	.75	33
.98	.001	.30	37

[1] (1 - SL)(Q/D)
[2] (1 - SL)(D/Q)
[3] $Z(\sigma_{LT})$

Forecasting models often used the mean absolute deviation (MAD) instead of the standard deviation (σ_{LT}) to indicate the dispersion of the distribution of demand during lead time. Since the MAD is approximately equal to 1.25 time the σ_{LT} the relationships shown in Exhibit 3-6 can be used for either measuring or determining the required level of safety stock to be added to expected demand in order to calculate the reorder point.

Exhibit 3-6
Table of Service Levels, Z values and MAD Values

Service Level (1 - P(S))	No. of σs (Z values)	No. of MADs
.999	3.09	3.86
.990	2.33	2.91
.980	2.05	2.56
.975	1.96	2.45
.950	1.64	2.06
.900	1.28	1.60
.850	1.04	1.30
.800	.85	1.05
.750	.67	.84

Other models are available to calculate reorder points for other service level definitions and for where the forecast interval and the lead time interval are not equal. Examples of these models are provided in the inventory management texts listed in the bibliography to this study.

Fixed Period Approach

As described in Chapter 2, in the fixed period approach to ordering inventory, the inventory position is reviewed at predetermined intervals and a decision is made to place an order or not. The size of any order (the "how much" decision) is determined by subtracting the amount on hand from a predetermined level. The order interval and the predetermined level completely define the fixed period inventory approach.

Example

A financial institution uses a substantial volume of forms. As part of the service agreement, the vendor agreed to stock those forms (with safety stock) based on anticipated next month's usage. Each month, the institution places an order for next month based on anticipated need. These are released on a weekly basis or as actual need dictates. Thus, the vendor is carrying most of the inventory for the institution.

The total cost of the fixed period approach is a function of the length of the review period and the predetermined maximum level. In practice, the review period tends to be selected based on factors such as the number of clerks available to inspect stock, or is fixed at some convenient period such as weeks or months.

Model 1 — Single Item Economic Order Intervals

Optimal economic order intervals rarely are calculated for individual items. However, using the following equations, order intervals may be calculated based on costs by relating the order quantity to the order interval.

$$Q \quad = \quad DT \qquad \qquad \text{(Equation 3.9)}$$

Where:

Q = order quantity,

D = annual demand, and

T = order interval as a proportion of the year.

If Q = EOQ, then EOQ = DT, and T = EOQ/D.　　　　(Equation 3.10)

As an example, if the EOQ equals 1,000 units and annual demand equals 10,000 units, the optimal order interval would be 1,000/10,000 or .10 years. If there are 250 working days, the review period would be every 25 days.

Model 2 — Multiple Item Economic Order Intervals

Economic order intervals are more likely to be calculated where one supplier provides numerous items. It is more economical to have joint orders since inventory maintenance may be kept to a minimum and transportation cost savings are possible.

The economic order interval for a family of items may be found by using the next equation.

$$T = \sqrt{\frac{2(S + n(O))}{I \sum_{i=i}^{n} D_i \ C_i}}$$

(Equation 3.11)

where:

i = ith family of items,

S = ordering cost per order,

n = number of items,

I = carrying cost expressed as a percent,

O = ordering cost per item,

C_i = cost for the ith family, and

D_i = annual demand for the ith family

Suppose a firm orders six items from the same vendor. The ordering costs are $2 per order and 50 cents per item. Given a carrying cost of 20% per year and the following data on the six items, what is the minimum cost order interval.

Item	Annual Demand	Ordering Cost Per Unit	Total Ordering Costs
1	200	$1.50	$ 300
2	400	.50	200
3	300	3.00	900
4	125	1.00	125
5	175	1.00	175
6	400	2.00	800
			$2,500

The minimum cost order interval is found by solving Equation 3.11 as follows:

$$T = \sqrt{\frac{2(2.00 + 6(.50))}{.20(2500)}} = .141 \text{ years}$$

or every 51 days.

The assumptions underlying this model are the same as those underlying the basic EOQ model described in Chapter 2. These models are relatively insensitive to parameter estimates and may provide good approximate solutions to determining the optimal order interval for a fixed period approach.

Single Period Models

The fixed quantity and fixed period models presented in Chapter 2 and thus far in Chapter 3 have assumed that the reordering process was continuous; that is, items are ordered and stocked with the expectation that the need would continue. Some inventory situations involve ordering to cover only one demand period or ordering to cover short-lived items at frequent intervals. These situations frequently occur for retail and wholesale customer goods.

Example

A manufacturer of rubber products would purchase a whole shipload of raw rubber at one time. As the ship unloaded, the manufacturer sold excess requirements on the spot market. By ordering in this fashion, it was able to provide some degree of reliability in delivery. Over a period of time the gains and losses on the sale of the excess rubber almost canceled each other. Thus, there was no accounting profit or loss from such a strategy.

The optimal stocking decision may be found through marginal analysis of the benefits derived from carrying the next unit and of the costs for that unit. The optimal stocking level is to stock the quantity where the profit from the sale of that last unit is greater than or equal to the loss of that unit not being sold. When demand is uncertain, we are looking at expected profits and expected losses. The following "newsboy" problem may be used to illustrate this model.

Suppose a news carrier takes along a few extra papers on his/her route. For the past few months, the carrier has kept a record of how many times he/she has been asked for extra papers when on the route. This record is presented in the table on page 58.

If there were no uncertainty, the problem would be simple; the carrier would carry the extra papers demanded.

Another factor to be considered, in addition to the uncertainty of demand, is the profit that will be realized on the sale of a paper. The higher that profit, the more papers it will be worthwhile to carry.

Frequency and Probability of Sales

Number of Extra Papers That Could Be Sold	Frequency	Probability	
		Noncumulative	Cumulative (less than)
0	2	.02	.00
1	7	.07	.02
2	15	.15	.09
3	20	.20	.24
4	18	.18	.44
5	16	.16	.62
6	10	.10	.78
7	7	.07	.88
8	3	.03	.95
9	1	.01	.98
10	1	.01	.99
11	0	.00	1.00
	100	1.00	

Conversely, if there is little or no profit on the sale of these extra papers, it will not be worthwhile to carry them and to incur the risk of not selling them.

For the sake of illustration, assume that the nonreimbursable cost of a paper is two cents and that the selling price is 10 cents; thus a profit of eight cents is made on each paper sold and a loss of two cents is incurred for each paper not sold. Because the actual sales and profits are not known until after the event, the best approach is to maximize expected profits. What policy can be adopted here that will maximize expected profits? First, suppose the carrier purchased enough extra papers to satisfy the average number of requests for extra papers, i.e., four. In the next table, the net profit from carrying these four extra papers is computed as the difference between the realized profit (eight cents per paper sold) and lost (two cents on each paper out of four that is not sold); the expected profit is the sum of the net profits weighted (multiplied) by the probability established for each possible outcome.

This expected profit of 24 cents is not the actual profit that will occur on any one trip. Indeed, it cannot occur on any one trip since, as may be seen from the net profit column, no particular number of requests for papers will result in a net profit of 24 cents. However, if the carrier were to carry four extra papers on all trips assuming that

Expected Profit from Carrying Four Extra Papers

Sales	Net Profit	Probability	Net Profit x Probability
0	-$.08	.02	-$.0016
1	.02	.07	.0014
2	.12	.15	.0180
3	.22	.20	.0440
4	.32	.56	.1792
Expected profit			$.2410

the probability distribution of selling extra papers is correct, the average net profit per trip over a period of time would be close to 24 cents.

There are two reasons why the expected profit will be less than the 32 cents which would be the profit on the average number of extra papers requested ($.08 x 4). First, the average number of realized sales per trip will be lower than the average number of requests (possible sales), unless the carrier has enough papers to meet all possible sales. Because there are only four papers, the carrier cannot realize any greater number of sales even though more people ask for additional papers, and because the carrier will sometimes sell less than that, the average sales will be fewer than four papers. Second, whenever the sales fall below four units, not only will a profit not be received on some of the papers but a loss of two cents will be incurred on any papers not sold.

Will the expected profit be at the highest level at four papers or are there other combinations that will earn more than 24 cents on the average? The expected profit for various decisions about the number of extra papers to carry is:

Number of Extra Papers Carried	Expected Profit	Change in Expected Profit
4	$0.241	
5	0.259	$0.018
6	0.261	0.002
7	0.253	-0.008

Apparently, the optimum or maximum profit policy is to carry six extra papers, because the expected profit of 26 cents will then be at a maximum.

The complexities of the above analysis are too great and the calculations too extensive to be readily useful. However, a much simpler solution can be derived by using the marginal (incremental) approach.

In the final column of the table above appears the change in expected profit that results from carrying an additional paper. The fifth paper would bring an increase of .018 cents, the sixth paper an increase of two cents, whereas a seventh paper would reduce expected profit by .008 cents. The criterion for picking the optimum number of papers to carry can, therefore, be stated in two ways:

1. In terms of the total expected profit; and
2. In terms of the expected profit realized by carrying one paper more (incremental profit).

By using this incremental profit approach, a more general solution can be derived that permits a rapid determination of the best quantity to stock without making detailed computations of the expected profit for a number of units. The solution relates the probability of *not* selling the last unit to a "critical ratio," $C_2/(C_1 + C_2)$ as follows:

$$P(U < j) \quad < C_2 / (C_1 + C_2) \qquad \text{(Equation 3.12)}$$

where:

j	refers to the last unit (the number of the last extra paper in our illustration) to be carried,
U	refers to the number of such units that would have been sold had enough been available to meet all requests for them,
$P(U < j)$	refers to the probability that the number of extra units that could be sold is less than the last unit carried; i.e., it is the probability that the j paper will not be sold.
C_2	refers to the lost profit from not having a paper that could be sold, and
C_1	refers to the penalty for carrying a unit (paper) that is not sold.

According to this inequality, the paper carrier should continue to add to the stock of papers until the probability of *not* selling the last paper (the j paper) is just less than the ratio $C_2 / (C_1 + C_2)$. Substituting the figures in the previous example:

$$P(U < j) < C_2 / (C_1 + C_2)$$
$$< .08 / (.02 + .08)$$
$$< .8.$$

The stock of extra papers should be increased to the point where the probability of *not* selling the last paper is just less than .8. From the previous table of cumulative probabilities of selling various quantities of papers, the sixth paper is the highest extra paper for which the probability of its not being sold (.78) is less than .8.

The inequality confirms the conclusion reached in the previous illustration; the carrier should carry six extra papers on the route. The inequality, moreover, provides a quick means of reaching that conclusion, which is essential if an analysis of comparable complexity is to be applied to a realistic inventory situation.

Survey Results

As with the setting of order quantities, most respondents rely on experience in deciding safety stock, service levels and reorder points. As shown in Exhibit 3-7, a relatively small percentage of the respondents indicated that safety stocks are determined with the use of quantitative models. The combined low percentage for work-in-process (WIP) safety stocks may indicate that most firms carry safety stocks in raw materials and finished goods. Nonmanufacturer respondents indicated even less frequent use of quantitative models than did manufacturing.

Exhibit 3-7
Survey Frequency of Use of Quantitative Models and Experience in
Establishing Safety Stock Levels

Inventory	Method for Establishing Safety Stock	
	Quantitative Model	Experience
Manufacturing Respondents		
Raw Materials	33.3%	66.7%
Work-in-process	22.0	38.0
Finished Goods (and		
Merchandise)	32.6	86.5
Supplies	9.6	57.7
Service Parts	15.4	63.5
Nonmanufacturing		
Supplies	7.1	21.4
Service Parts	3.6	10.7
Merchandise (and		
Finished Goods)	28.5	89.3

Exhibit 3-8 indicates that nonmanufacturers, as well as manufacturers, use service level policies for their inventories. Finished goods (merchandise) is the most common area in which service level policies are applied, although raw materials are also monitored and managed using such a technique.

For the relatively small number of firms using the fixed time period inventory management system, the most frequent review periods are one week for all inventories except supplies and service parts, which are frequently four to 13 weeks. These review periods are determined by the organization's normal review period.

Exhibit 3-8
Survey Frequency of Use of Service Level Policies

Inventory	Frequency
Manufacturing Respondents	
Raw Materials	48.7%
Work-in-process	17.9
Finished Goods (and Merchandise)	82.1
Supplies	23.1
Service Parts	38.5
Nonmanufacturing Respondents	
Supplies	46.7
Service Parts	13.3
Merchandise (and Finished Goods)	48.4

Summary

The decision of when to order revolves primarily around balancing the carrying costs of safety stock with the stockout costs of not carrying sufficient safety stock. Quantitative models are presented that establish the reorder point by minimizing the sum of these costs, or that provide a service-level probability of satisfying inventory demand under varying conditions.

The survey results indicate the percent of respondents using quantitative models is relatively low. Further, except for finished goods (or merchandise) inventories, relatively few firms use service-level policies or base these policies on balancing stockout and carrying costs. Relatively few firms responded that they use the fixed time period approach, but those that did indicated their review period is determined by an organizational review schedule.

The relatively infrequent use of quantitative and statistical models indicates a significant gap between inventory management theory and inventory management practice. Many, if not most, of the companies use experience and intuition, which may be inferior when compared to statistical methods in setting safety stock levels. Experience rarely reflects the interrelated impacts on desired safety stock levels of forecast errors, lead time variations, order quantity sizes, and desired service levels.

Chapter 4

Dependent Demand Inventory Systems

The inventory models presented in Chapters 2 and 3 are known as independent demand inventory systems. These models are appropriate for managing inventories when the underlying assumptions about demand, lead time, order replenishment rate, and relevant costs hold. The crucial assumption for all of these types of models relates to the independence of demand for the item and implies a separate demand for each item which is unrelated to that of other items.

In a manufacturing system or in a multilevel distribution network, the demand for an item occurs because of the demand for "higher level" items. Raw material, work-in-process, and component items demand depend on the production schedule of the finished goods. Even if the level of demand for a finished product is constant, the need for the raw materials and subassemblies comprising this finished product only occurs at the time production is scheduled. Thus, the demand for the ingredients of a finished good is seldom constant. Add to this the complications of fluctuating demand for finished goods and the problem of complex product structures, where raw materials may be used in more than one product at different levels of manufacturing, and managing manufacturing inventories becomes a very difficult problem. Similarly, the demand for finished goods at a manufacturing site depends on the warehouse and retail inventory stocking policies.

These examples illustrate that the nature of dependent demand is different from that of independent demand inventory. In this chapter, the impact of this difference on independent demand models is illustrated, and a system for managing dependent demand inventories, called Materials (or Manufacturing) Requirements (or Resources) Planning (MRP) is presented.

Nature of Dependent Demand

In hierarchical (multilevel) inventory systems, two types of demand are present — dependent and independent. The demand of items at the highest level determines the demand or requirements of items at lower levels. The higher level demand is usually related to finished goods and the lower level demand is usually related to components, work-in-process and raw materials.

Exhibit 4-1
Independent Demand Versus Dependent Demand

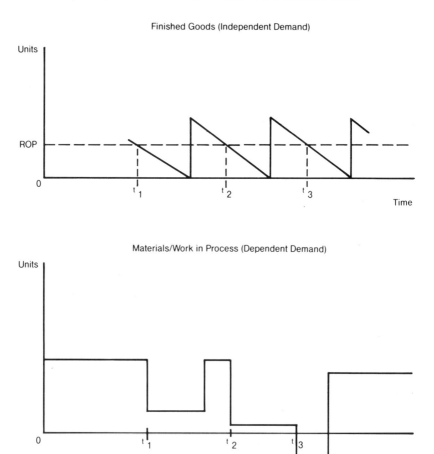

Finished Goods (Independent Demand)

Independent Demand

This type of demand is external to the firm and is changed by sales of a product. This demand may be influenced by advertising and marketing efforts with management reacting to meet an anticipated need of customers. The management and control of independent demand items (finished goods) may be accomplished by using the fixed quantity or fixed period type models presented in Chapters 2 and 3. The system chosen should be the one that most clearly satisfies the underlying assumptions about the flow of inventory. If the demand for finished goods is rather constant, perhaps an economic order quantity (EOQ) type of system is best. If the demand fluctuates from period to period, a fixed period, variable quantity system may be used. The choice of system will dictate when and how much of a finished good will be scheduled for production. Thus, the requirements for replenishment of finished goods drives the requirements of work-in-process, raw materials, and other factors of production. The requirements for these factors of production are dependent upon the stocking policies for finished goods.

Dependent Demand

The demand for a raw material or work-in-process item is derived from the demand for the finished good and usually follows the pattern shown in Exhibit 4-1.

Assuming a fixed order quantity replenishment model for the finished goods, production orders should be placed at time periods t_1, t_2, and t_3. The requirements for materials to produce the finished goods only occur when replenishment (production) orders for the finished goods occur. The inventory level of the materials is constant until t_1, t_2, and t_3 when a lot size of these materials (if they are available) is withdrawn, usually all at once, to support the production order quantity of the finished good.

As illustrated in Exhibit 4-1, the inventory level of the material fluctuates widely. At period t_3, the material available may not be sufficient to support the replenishment order for the finished good. At other times, the material level may be carried unnecessarily. Thus, the demand (requirements) of dependent items may be characterized as lumpy, or discontinuous, and derived from the inventory restocking policies of higher or next level items. Changes in the restocking policies of the higher level item and uncertainties in the order lead time of the dependent demand item result in wide fluctuations in the inventory level of the dependent demand item. If independent demand models as described in Chapters 2 and 3 are used to manage these items, incorrect ordering decisions may cause orders to be placed too soon or too late, resulting in high levels of inventory and high stockouts. The impact of using inappropriate independent demand inventory models for dependent demand items may be illustrated with the following example using Part X to produce a finished good.

Case 1

Assume the following:
   1. Past demand has averaged 18 units per week.
   2. Lead time has averaged three weeks.
   3. The desired safety stock is 20 units.
   4. Inventory on hand is 80 units.
   5. The finished good production requirements are 55, 40, and 15 for weeks one, five, and six, respectively.

Using the reorder point model, the reorder point for Part X would equal

$$ROP = \text{Lead time (average demand)} + \text{Safety stock}$$
$$= 3(18) + 20$$
$$= 74 \text{ units.}$$

During week one, 55 units of Part X would be withdrawn from inventory and the inventory level (80−55) would fall below the ROP (74). Moreover, because weekly demand averages 18 units, the 25 available units of Part X would not support the average demand for the three weeks' order lead time of Part X. Thus, the order would be rushed or expedited to arrive in week two. However, the correct action would be to wait until week two to place a replenishment order of Part X because there are no requirements for the item until week five.

Case 2

The same facts apply for Part X except that on-hand inventory equals 40 (not 80) and 100 units of Part X are on order to arrive in week three. Using the reorder point system, the inventory available in period one equals on-hand (40) plus on order (100) minus demand

(55), or 85 units. Because 85 units is above the reorder point of 74, no action would be taken. However, the actual available inventory for period one is 40−55 or − 15 units and an order should be expedited immediately.

These cases illustrate the impact of lumpy demand on reorder point models. This impact is exacerbated when production orders for higher level items are changed, when replenishment order lead times change, and when common parts are used in multiple higher level items. It is because of these problems that manufacturing companies have used fixed period, variable quantity approaches to managing dependent demand items. However, these systems are different from those presented in Chapters 2 and 3 in that future requirements are not forecasted but are calculated based on planned production of higher level items. Because of the large number of items and the complex interdependency of these items, MRP systems are computer based in all but the smallest and simplest of manufacturing environments.

Example

A manufacturer of small motors installed an MRP system in two phases. During the first phase, all "A" items were put on the computerized MRP system. Remaining items were controlled with a weekly period review system. The first phase was a total disaster because several of the parts that were not included in the MRP program had long lead times and were used in many different subassemblies. To correct this problem, the firm ordered the difference in on-hand inventories and a quarter's average usage every week. This was almost 12 weeks of safety stock, but it reduced stockouts completely.

MRP Systems Overview

Definition and Assumptions

The definition and meaning of MRP has evolved over the last two decades from a limited perspective of a data processing logic block to calculating material requirements for an integrated manufacturing management information and decision support system. Underlying these definitions are the following common assumptions.

1. Dependent demands of materials are driven by production

schedules of independent demand items. An MRP system is built upon this concept of dependent demand; the system is driven by the production scheduled to meet the demand for the finished goods. Remember that the assumption of constant demand is critical to the traditional EOQ system. It is not important to the fixed period, variable quantity system and, by implication, the MRP system. This relaxation of the constant demand assumption ties many manufacturing systems more closely to the reality — that of fluctuating demand.

2. Inventory and production scheduling decisions are based on the future and not the past. An MRP system makes inventory decisions based on planned usage and not actual usage. In the traditional EOQ system, inventory is not replenished until an ROP is reached — based on actual usage. The MRP system replenishes material and schedules production based on anticipated demand of the finished goods. The demand for finished goods is monitored and adjustments are made to production schedules and inventory levels as conditions warrant. Like the fixed period system from which it is derived, the MRP system is a forward-looking inventory management and control system. MRP anticipates future needs and reacts to this anticipated future need. The traditional EOQ system reacts to historical events, or actual usage, and does not anticipate demands that may happen in the future. The probability models of the EOQ systems are geared to prevent unpleasant events from occurring rather than reacting by taking action to avoid these events. For example, an EOQ system may use a high level of safety stock in order to meet fluctuations in demand while the MRP system would anticipate when such demands may occur and react to meet these future needs.

3. Computerized data and information processing are necessary and available. The development and use of MRP systems follow the evolution and development of the computer itself. As will be illustrated in a later section of this chapter, an MRP system requires processing large databases. First, however, a discussion of the evolution of such a system indicates why such large databases are needed.

Evolution of MRP

MRP is not a new concept. The idea of managing material requirements based on anticipated needs has been understood and applied since production endeavors have been undertaken. What is new, however, is the ability to apply the concept to complex, large scale problems in rapidly changing environments. The commercial availability of high-capacity computers and software programs provided an ability to use the MRP concept. In 1970, at the annual meeting of the American Production and Inventory Control Society (APICS), engineers from IBM presented a paper describing a materials requirements planning system.[1] From this beginning, the explosive growth in applications of such systems started. This approach is now in the third generation, and continued evolution is expected.[2]

First Generation of MRP

The first generation of MRP was labeled a material requirements planning system and was concerned with the acquisition and use of raw materials in a manufacturing environment. The definition and meaning of MRP was conceptually limited to a computerized data processing system which used bills of material, inventory data, and master production schedules to calculate requirements for materials. Recommended replenishment and rescheduled orders were the primary outputs of this generation of MRP. Material requirements were time phased based on needs and were determined using bills of material. Accountants have long used bills of material in developing standard costs but not in inventory management and control. In an MRP system using a bill of materials, the needs for materials are exploded through the levels of manufacturing.

Material requirements may be calculated using the following equation:

$$NR_t = GR_t - SR_t - OH_t \qquad \text{(Equation 4.1)}$$

Where
NR = net requirements,
GR = gross requirements,
SR = scheduled receipts,
OH = on-hand inventory, and
t = the time period.

The net requirements indicate the material requirements needed in a period to meet the higher level production plans and are used to make decisions of when and how much to order. The order lead time for the item is used to time phase planned orders to satisfy the net requirements.

Because the master production schedule of the independent demand item (level 0 item) is the gross requirement for the next level (level one) dependent demand items, the planned order releases of the level one items become the gross requirements of the level two items, and so on until the net requirements and planned orders are determined for all materials at all levels.

In the example shown in Exhibit 4-2, inventory ordered (planned order release) is the exact amount required at the times required. This is called a lot-for-lot ordering policy. Other ordering policies will be presented in later sections.

In the example below, the need for materials at level two is dependent

Exhibit 4-2
Illustration of MRP Logic

Item		Period								
		1	2	3	4	5	6	7	8	9
A	Gross Requirements	10		15	10	20	5		10	15
Level = 0	Scheduled Receipts			14						
	On Hand = 12	2	2	1						
LT = 1	Net Requirements				9	20	5		10	15
	Planned Order Receipts				9	20	5		10	15
	Planned Order Release			9	20	5		10	15	
B	Gross Requirements			9	20	5		10	15	
Level = 1	Scheduled Receipts									
	On Hand = 28	28	28	19						
LT = 2	Net Requirements				1	5		10	15	
	Planned Order Receipts				1	5		10	15	
	Planned Order Release	1	5		10	15				
C	Gross Requirements	1	5		10	15				
Level = 2	Scheduled Receipts									
	On Hand = 8	8	7	2	2					
LT = 2	Net Requirements				8	15				
	Planned Order Receipts				8	15				
	Planned Order Release	8	15							

upon the planned orders for materials at level one which, in turn, are dependent upon the planned orders at level 0. One may follow the data flows in Exhibit 4-2 for an example of this. Note that the total gross requirements of 85 units of item A only require an item C total of 23 units to be ordered. An MRP system explodes the need for materials by the bill of materials and planned production schedule, nets out the scheduled receipts and on-hand inventory, and then time phases these needs by "buckets" of time.

There are several features of such an inventory management system. The first is that the concept is a variation of a fixed period, variable quantity system with one notable difference. The need for materials is based on the products to be produced and traced through the various levels of manufacturing. A traditional fixed-period, variable quantity system does not explode requirements through manufacturing levels.

The second notable feature is that this is one of the first computer-based inventory systems. Because frequent revisions of large masses of data are necessary, the data processing requirements are such that a manual system is not normally feasible. An MRP system is one of the earliest business application computer success stories.

Third, the first generation MRP system ties together the planned sales and production of finished goods with material requirements. Production and inventory planning of finished goods, work-in-process, and raw materials are integrated and require a high degree of coordination between purchasing, marketing, and production. There are several features that are not included in a first-generation MRP system which, in turn, led to the development of the second generation.

Example

A vendor in Cleveland has an MRP system integrated with the MRP system of a manufacturer. As a strike developed at the location of the manufacturer, the two MRP systems were able to coordinate the immediate future needs and the vendor was able to slow or in some cases cancel shipments from suppliers to the vendor. The vendor was also, in a few cases, able to rearrange and speed up production for some other items so that when the strike was settled, a large part of the production capacity was devoted to this one manufacturer for a short period of time. By integrating these two systems, the vendor was able to escape serious problems because of the strike at the location of the manufacturer.

Second Generation of MRP

Another name for the second generation of MRP is MRP II. This system is also called a Closed Loop Materials Requirement Planning System or a Manufacturing Resource Planning System and is illustrated in Exhibit 4-3.

Exhibit 4-3
MRP II
Closed Loop Manufacturing System

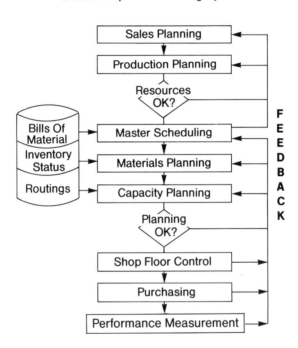

In this version of MRP, capacity planning is integrated with materials and labor planning, and all efforts are coordinated. The emphasis in such a system is on planning and accountability. All the factors in a firm become an integral part of the planning and control process.

Third Generation of MRP

An MRP system, as such, is expressed in quantities and not dollars.

Thus, the traditional MRP systems may not be integrated with the standard cost systems and, in some companies, the standard cost of a product may be determined by accounting standards and the method of production by engineering standards. Accounting and engineering standards may or may not agree with each other. The third generation of MRP systems incorporates and integrates the accounting systems into the MRP systems so that the accounting and engineering standards are reconciled and integrated with the various reporting systems.

Distribution Requirements Planning (DRP)

The MRP concepts also apply to distribution inventories. Dependent demand characterizes retail and wholesale distribution networks as well as warehousing and physical distribution networks within a manufacturing company. Lumpy demand may occur at a central production facility (or warehouse) because of lot sizing and reorder points at the distribution centers (or retailers). Using reactive reorder points at the production facility (or warehouse) for finished goods in these hierarchical systems will result in the same problems identified earlier for dependent demand in work-in-process and raw material items.

These problems can be handled using DRP. The logic is exactly the same as with MRP. Gross requirements are calculated at the highest level in the hierarchy or the stocking point that satisfies the customer demand. These gross requirements are then netted out for existing inventory and offset for lead times to generate planned order releases. These planned order releases become the gross requirements at the supplying inventory point in the network (or the next level in the hierarchy). The netting out and time phasing process is repeated at the successive inventory stocking points in the network.

MRP Decision Variables

The two basic decisions of inventory management, how much and when to order or produce, must still be addressed in an MRP system. The net requirements indicate the inventory amount that must be received by some time period to meet the planned production requirements of a higher-level item. The net requirements calculated each period in the MRP system are analogous to the demand forecasted each period in the fixed quantity and fixed period models presented

in Chapters 2 and 3. Decisions of how much and when to order or produce to meet these calculated net requirements should be made so
that inventory carrying and ordering costs are minimized.

As illustrated in the discussion of the fixed period inventory system,
the question of when to order is based upon periods of time. A review
is made at the end of the selected period and a decision is made at
that time as to whether to place an order or not. In an MRP system,
the question then is what time buckets are used for exploding and
time phasing material requirements.

There are four popular methods of determining how much to produce
or order. Each of these methods determines the number of periods of
net requirements to be ordered and, therefore, indicates when orders
will be placed. The four methods are:

1.   Lot-for-lot, which generates planned orders in quantities
      equal to the net requirements offset by the lead time,
2.   Economic order quantity, which generates planned orders
      using the basic EOQ model,
3.   Economic review period, which generates planned orders
      to cover economic review periods or that period of time
      that average demand is satisfied by the EOQ,
4.   Part-period balancing, which generates planned orders
      to minimize ordering and carrying costs by calculating a
      lot quantity and before it is firmed up, the next or the
      previous periods' demands are evaluated to verify
      whether it would be economical to include them in the
      current lot.

These four methods may be illustrated with the following problem.
Assume Part X has the following gross requirements, a lead time of
one week, and inventory on hand of 30 units.

	Period											
Part X	1	2	3	4	5	6	7	8	9	10	11	12
Gross requirements	25	15	10	0	14	0	7	12	40	7	15	5

Also assume a carrying cost of $1.50 per unit per week and an order-
ing cost of $45 per order.

The net requirements for Part X are as follows:

	Period											
Part X	1	2	3	4	5	6	7	8	9	10	11	12
Gross requirements	25	15	10	0	14	0	7	12	40	7	15	5
On hand = 30	5											
Net requirements		10	10	0	14	0	7	12	40	7	15	5

Lot-for-Lot Ordering Rule

The ordering policy for this rule is to order the net requirements when they are needed. Thus, each period's net requirements would be ordered one week (the lead time) in advance. There would be nine orders placed and no inventory carried (other than the five units in period one carried over from initial on-hand inventory). The relevant costs of this policy are:

$$TC = (9 \times \$45) + (0 \times \$1.50) = \$405.00.$$

Economic Order Quantity Ordering Rule (EOQ)

The EOQ ordering rule attempts to balance ordering and carrying costs. The EOQ rule assumes requirements are constant over time and uses the basic EOQ formula as follows:

$$EOQ = \sqrt{2DS / CI}$$
$$= \sqrt{2(10)(45) / 1.50}$$
$$= 25 \text{ units.}$$

Where D = average weekly demand;
= sum net requirements / 12 = 10

Using this ordering rule, the inventory level can be shown in the following MRP format, depicted on the next page.

	Period											
Part X	1	2	3	4	5	6	7	8	9	10	11	12
Gross requirements	25	15	10	0	14	0	7	12	40	7	15	5
On hand = 30	5	15	5	5	16	16	9	22	7	0	10	5
Net requirements	0	10*	0	0	9*	0	0	3*	18*	0	15*	0
Planned order receipts	0	25	0	0	25	0	0	25	25	0	25	0
Planned order releases	25	0	0	25	0	0	25	25	0	25	0	0

The starred net requirements signal a reorder quantity requirement. For this rule, five orders are placed and 110 units are carried in inventory (beyond the five units in period one) for a total cost of:

$$TC = (5 \times \$45) + (110 \times \$1.50) = \$390.00.$$

Economic Review Period Ordering Rule

The economic review period ordering rule expresses the order quantity as equal to the net requirements covered by the economic number of periods to be covered by the order. The economic number of periods is the number of periods divided by the economic number of orders. For this problem, the economic number of orders is the sum of the net requirements (120) divided by the EOQ (25), or 4.8 orders. The economic number of periods equals 12 periods divided by 4.8 orders or 2.5 periods. Rounding up and using a three-period review ordering results in the following inventory levels.

	Period											
Part X	1	2	3	4	5	6	7	8	9	10	11	12
Gross requirements	25	15	10	0	14	0	7	12	40	7	15	
			0	14	0	0	52	40	0	20	5	0
Net requirements	0	0	0	0	0	0	0	0	0	0	0	0
Planned order receipts	0	0	0	14	0	0	59	0	0	27	0	0
Planned order releases	0	0	14	0	0	59	0	0	27	0	0	0

In the above example, it is assumed that scheduled orders of 20 units have been ordered prior to period one to make up the difference in gross requirements of 50 units for periods one, two, and three and on-hand inventory of 30 units. For this ordering rule, four orders would be placed in each 12-period cycle and 161 units (beyond the five units in period one) are carried in inventory for a total cost of:

TC = (4 x $45) + (161 x $1.50) = $421.50.

Part-Period Balancing Ordering Rule

The part-period balancing ordering rule is a trial-and-error approach to minimizing ordering and carrying costs. Unlike the previous two rules based on the EOQ formula, there is no assumption about constant demand. The idea is to find the number of part-periods that balance the cost of ordering against the cost of carrying. A part-period is defined as one part held in inventory for one period. The economic part-period is equal to the ratio of ordering costs to carrying cost. For this problem, the economic part-period is $45 / $1.50 = 30 part-periods. The mechanics of the calculations of the ordering quantities are beyond the scope of this report. However, the results of this ordering rule are shown below.

		Period										
Part X	1	2	3	4	5	6	7	8	9	10	11	12
Gross requirements	25	15	10	0	14	0	7	12	40	7	15	5
On hand = 30	5	10	0	0	7	7	0	0	7	0	5	0
Planned order receipts	0	20	0	0	21	0	0	12	47	0	20	0
Planned order releases	20	0	0	21	0	0	12	47	0	20	0	0

Five orders are placed and 36 units (beyond the five units in period one) are carried in inventory for a total cost of:

TC = (5 x $45) + (36 x $1.50) = $279.00.

Comparison of the Ordering Rules

A review of the total costs as calculated for each of the decision rules, using a given demand pattern, indicates that the part-period balancing ordering rule is the best minimum cost rule given this demand pattern. This will always be the case unless the net requirements are sufficiently constant over time to meet the underlying assumption of the EOQ-based model.

The four rules represent varying levels of complexity to use, with the lot-for-lot being the simplest and the part-period balancing being the most complex. However, all these rules are available in most computerized MRP programs.

The lot-for-lot rule carries the least inventory and smoothes the flow of work for lower level items. A review of the order sizes and frequencies in the above problem shows how the other rules combine the net requirements of periods for fewer orders. This means that rules other than lot-for-lot will explode these combined net requirements down through the bill of materials and increase the gross requirements of lower level dependent items.

MRP Implementation Issues

Most medium- and large-size manufacturing companies have or are in the process of installing computerized MRP. Successful implementations report the following benefits: reduced inventory, better delivery performance, reduced idle time, reduced setup time, quicker and better response to changes, better customer service, reduced sales prices, and increased sales. Increased competition has motivated more and more firms to adopt systems, including MRP, to realize these benefits. Yet the landscape is covered with MRP "failures" or those that have not fully captured the potential benefits cited above. What explains these failures of a proven system? The answer to this question rests in part with technical issues but mostly with organizational and behavioral issues.

Technical Issues

There are three technical issues that must be resolved. They are record accuracy, regeneration method, and safety stock levels. Accurate bills of material and inventory records are a must for a successful MRP system. Often, bills of material do not reflect either the product structure or the manufacturing processes of the product. Over time, based on experience, modifications are made to improve the original product and/or process designs. Updated bills of material may not exist to reflect these modifications.

Similarly, actual physical inventory levels may not be consistent with inventory records. Many companies have open stockrooms where inventory can be withdrawn by anyone needing materials. Periodic inventory counting is then used to reconcile inventory record discrepancies. With MRP systems, these approaches will not work, inasmuch as daily assurance of inventory integrity is an absolute must for successful MRP systems.

The regeneration question revolves around how often and how the MRP should be run to reflect changes. Running the MRP involves preparing a new schedule for production and material needs. After a change occurs, should the MRP be rerun? Should the entire MRP be rerun or only those parts affected by the change?

Too frequent regeneration is costly from a data processing point of view and may result in system nervousness or overreaction. Biweekly, weekly, or monthly regeneration would seem to be the most reasonable choices.

Ordinarily, the regeneration method used is a complete rerun of the MRP. Some software programs provide a net change method, which only updates those parts of the system and those reports and schedules affected by the change.

As discussed in previous chapters, safety stock is or should be used to prevent unplanned stockouts. Theoretically, since the production and purchases are based on anticipated or planned sales in an MRP system, there should be little, if any, need for safety stock and the level of safety stock should approach zero. As a practical matter, because of all the uncertainties involved in an inventory system, most MRP implementations do plan for safety stocks. The question to be answered is where this safety stock should be maintained.

There is little rationale for carrying safety stock in all three inventory categories when safety stock in any inventory class may provide the needed protection against unplanned stockouts. Safety stock is sometimes provided by overplanning. Since the MRP system considers the safety stock a fixed quantity, overplanning at higher levels in the bills of material explodes this fixed quantity down through lower levels and results in higher safety stocks at lower levels than will ever actually be used.

It would seem reasonable to assume that if safety stock is to be maintained for raw materials, it would be desirable to have the vendor maintain the safety stock for the company. In essence, the vendor would be incurring the carrying cost.

Organizational and Behavioral Issues

The major obstacles to successful MRP implementation seem to be organizational and behavioral in nature. An MRP system is a "formal" system that requires the integration of production, marketing, finance, and personnel. Achieving integration of departmentalized efforts and tasks is an organizational theory conundrum that transcends the MRP system. However, an MRP system requires a high degree of coordination and integration, which many companies do not have organizational mechanisms to facilitate.

In addition, an MRP system will require changes in the behavior of all personnel involved. Job definitions and procedures must change vertically, as well as horizontally, and because MRP is a formal system, strict adherence to procedures is required. There is a natural resistance to change, particularly when the change is from a highly autonomous informal system to a highly structured formal system. Overcoming this resistance to change is probably the major challenge to successfully implementing a MRP system. White offers some suggestions on how to overcome such resistance.[3]

Example

A VP of manufacturing related a story of how his firm implemented an MRP system. One of the DP section managers read about MRP systems and the dramatic improvements made possible by a computerized package that could be purchased from a reliable software vendor. The DP manager convinced the VP that the system was essentially a data processing system that could be up and running in six months. All that was needed were a few additional programmers to convert the manual records into computerized records and about fifty thousand dollars to buy the software. Twenty-four months and a quarter of a million dollars later, the manufacturer was no closer to a computerized MRP system than day one.

Survey Results

Of the total number of questionnaires returned, 57 were from manufacturing companies. About 70% of these firms use some type of MRP system. MRP is used most often to manage raw materials (67.3%), less often with work-in-process (54.5%), and still less often with finished goods (52.7%). This indicates that most firms view MRP from a first-generation perspective of materials requirements explosion logic. Interestingly, over 85% of the respondents indicated that they did not plan to change their inventory systems in the near future. It appears there is no strong movement toward a second- or third-generation MRP system.

Approximately 20% of the manufacturing respondents and over 25% of the nonmanufacturing respondents reported they use a Distribution Requirements Planning (DRP) system. This result may be due to the type of warehousing systems used (few branch warehousing) or to the failure to time phase their finished goods. In the second case, where finished goods are not time phased, one may suppose that these firms are using a more traditional method of inventory management and control such as the EOQ system.

Of the four ordering rules, two accounted for over 68% of the methods used by the manufacturing companies that responded to the questionnaire. These two were the lot-for-lot and economic order quantity methods. The lot-for-lot method was the most widely accepted regardless of the level at which it was applied.

MRP and DRP respondents most frequently selected one week as the regeneration period or time period between runs of the MRP system (over 65%). Over 66% of the manufacturing respondents use full regeneration, while over 75% of the nonmanufacturing respondents used the net change method. This reflects the relative ease of using net change in a DRP application as opposed to an MRP application.

The maintenance of safety stock was almost evenly split between raw materials and end items for MRP manufacturing respondents. While some respondents maintain safety stock at all levels, over 50% of the firms have raw materials and finished goods safety stocks. Service parts safety stocks are maintained in over 40% of the firms, while no more than one out of four has WIP safety stocks. Over 85% of the DRP nonmanufacturing respondents carry finished goods safety stock.

When manufacturing respondents were asked to characterize the class of their MRP/DRP systems, "not certain" was the most frequent answer with over 41%. Less than 7% of the MRP systems are classified as "A" systems. This supports the earlier conclusion that *most* systems are first-generation MRP systems.

Summary

Materials and Distribution Requirements Planning (MRP/DRP) systems are designed to manage inventory in dependent demand environments. These systems have been developed since the original

NAA research report on inventory management and have been one of the most popular topics in production and inventory management over the past decade. During this period the definition of these systems has evolved from a narrow focus on exploding material requirements to a business planning focus on integrating all functional units in the organization.

The number of successful MRP/DRP implementations is a surprisingly small percentage of the large and increasing number of implementation attempts over the past decade. The major obstacle to successful implementation has not been technical problems, such as record accuracy, but instead has been the organizational and behavioral difficulties of overcoming resistance to change.

The survey results indicate that about 70% of the respondents use some type of MRP/DRP system to manage their inventories. Most of these systems are first generation systems and relatively few are class "A" systems. Over 85% of the respondents indicated no plans to change their inventory management systems, undoubtedly reflecting their desire to improve and refine systems that have had high financial and social costs.

Weekly time periods ("buckets") for planning and weekly review periods are used by over 65% of the respondents. Full regeneration was reported by over 66% of the manufacturing respondents while over 75% of the nonmanufacturing respondents reported the net change method. The lot-for-lot and economic order quantity rules were reported by over 68% of the respondents. Safety stocks are most frequently carried at the raw materials and finished goods levels.

Notes

[1] One of the early classic works in this area is a speech by Joseph A. Orlicky, G.W. Plossl, and O.W. Wright, titled "Material Requirements Planning System," presented at the 1970 APICS International Conference in Cincinnati.

[2] One of the earliest detailed presentations of the philosophy of the MRP, which expanded the concept to Manufacturing Requirements Planning, is found in Thurston, Philip H. "Requirements Planning for Inventory Control," *Harvard Business Review*, May-June 1972.

[3] White, Edna M. "Implementing an MRP System Using the Lewin-Schein Theory of Change", *Production and Inventory Management*, Vol. 21, No. 1, First Quarter 1980, pp. 1-2.

Chapter 5

Inventory Management Information Systems

Since the 1964 NAA study on inventory management and control, the most significant changes have occurred in the area of inventory management information systems.[1] These changes have been brought about by advancements in the commercial application of computers and computer-related technology to inventory management and control. This chapter describes the characteristics of inventory information systems; contrasts formal, computer systems with informal, manual systems; discusses the trend toward computerized systems; describes the relationships among databases, files, records, and information pyramids; discusses the subsystems of an inventory information system; and relates survey results to state-of-the-art applications of computer-based inventory management systems.

Characteristics of Inventory Management Information Systems

Functions of Systems

Inventory management information systems provide three basic functions:

1. Inventory data entry and record keeping.
2. Inventory data processing.
3. Inventory decision making and report generation.

Inventory data entry and record keeping have become a major expense for many companies. Data entry and record keeping historically have been manual operations, which are both time consuming and inherently inaccurate; thus, specialized computer entry devices have been developed. Examples of these devices include video display (VDT) and hand-held terminals, optical scanners, badge-reading terminals, bar code printers, and voice input devices. These devices reduce the errors and the time lags in record keeping that are related to recording inventory receipts and disbursements.

Inventory data processing activities range from simple arithmetic, such as subtracting disbursements from beginning inventory to calculate quantities on hand, to complex calculations, such as net change requirements for common raw materials in an MRP system. Having computerized inventory records and bills of material with computerized arithmetic instructions reduces data processing errors and time lags.

The primary function of the inventory management information system is to improve decision making. This is usually accomplished by generating reports that contain needed information for decisions and that also indicate the planned impact of decisions. As an example, information on past demand may be generated to be used in forecasting future demand, which in turn is used to decide how much to order. The planned order may then be used to generate a report showing projected inventory levels and cash flow needs. Inventory decision models, such as those provided in Chapters 2 through 4, have been computerized in a wide variety of organizations.

Formal Versus Informal Information Systems

Inventory management information systems are used to maintain inventory records and/or to develop inventory management decision information. While there are numerous definitions of the word "system," for our purposes we are referring to the logic by which inventory information is handled and the activities of inventory management as they are carried out using this information. In most organizations, inventory information and management activities use a complex set of formal and informal systems. Formal and informal systems may be characterized by the extreme points of a continuum as shown in Exhibit 5-1.

Exhibit 5-1
Informal Versus Formal Systems

Informal Systems	Formal Systems
←	→
Highly Personal	Highly Impersonal
Low Predictability	High Predictability
Low Reliability	High Reliability
Autonomous, Independent Decisions	Integrated, Company-wide Decisions

Example

A small retailer was experiencing rapid growth. The president decided that a computerized billing, accounts payable and receivable, purchasing, and inventory management system was needed. A widely publicized vendor sold the president a popular small business computer and supporting software. After one year of trying to install the system, the firm was still relying on the manual system.

What the president learned was that the firm's manual systems were not formalized and, as a result, could not be computerized. The president set about formalizing the functions to be computerized with standard operating procedures and forms. Once this was achieved, the computerized system paid for itself in one year in terms of the average billing and shipping cost per transaction.

Manual inventory management systems tend to be informal for the following reasons:

1. Formalizing manual systems is labor intensive and, therefore, costly.
2. Managers view flexibility as essential to control and management.
3. Managers perceive that achieving the high degree of integration required for formal systems is impractical for their organizations.

Computer-based inventory management systems are more formal for the following reasons:

1. Computer programs and records force explicit definitions and rigid logic in processing information.
2. The cost/performance curves of computers increasingly are allowing companies to integrate data and decision activities for company-wide management and control.
3. Control over information processing is greater with a computerized system.

The difference in a manual and computer system approach may be illustrated with a simple inventory and purchasing example. In the manual system, the following steps occur:

1. The inventory control clerk stocks materials and maintains an independent and separate inventory record.
2. When inventory appears to be getting low according to the records, purchasing is requested to develop purchase orders.
3. Purchase order copies are sent (eventually) to the inventory control clerk to be compared with inventory records.

The information is maintained and processed independently by the inventory control clerk and the buyer in purchasing. There are time lags in the back-and-forth communications and potential for data processing errors.

A computerized system could do the following:

1. Provide all back-and-forth communication virtually instantaneously between the inventory control clerk and the purchasing buyer.
2. Review all inventory records after the clerk enters receipts and issuances to inventory records.
3. List those materials that are needed and provide that information to the purchasing buyer.
4. Prepare purchase orders for the buyer and update inventory records to reflect quantities ordered.

For this computerized system, the system controls how records are kept and how purchase orders are produced. There are few or no communication time lags between inventory control and purchasing. The system is more predictable and has a higher reliability than a manual system, but it is less flexible. However, it does integrate the two related functions of when and how much to order.

Today's and the Future Environment

The 1980s have presented organizations with a new environment in which to manage inventories. Raw material and purchased parts availability and costs have become unpredictable. Labor availability, especially for skilled labor, and capital availability have become scarce, resulting in dramatic increases in the costs of acquiring these operating factors. Product life cycles have shortened and products are more complex to design, make, and sell. Computer hardware and software acquisition and application costs have declined to the point where even small firms can economically justify these investments. Lastly, the competitive environment has become more intense as a result of deregulation and foreign competition, as well as the other changes cited above.

Some companies have been able to achieve outstanding results during these turbulent times. Some of the successes related to inventory management include:

1. Dramatic reduction in inventory investment even though sales and per unit inventory costs have increased.
2. Significant reductions in customer service lead times.
3. Elimination of customer backorders.

In the aggregate, organizations are doing a better job of managing inventories than was the case in the 1970s. Aggregate inventories no longer fluctuate widely from over- and under-stocked conditions to the extent that was the norm for decades.

These results have not been achieved by managing inventories with the same old manual systems used for decades. Twenty years ago, production and inventory management and control was a clerical, statistically oriented task that was viewed as a rather minor technical part in overall business management. Traditional inventory management systems were almost exclusively informal and manual until the early 1970s.

The new environment has created an entirely new approach to managing in general and managing inventories in particular. This new approach is characterized by formal systems using integrated information with management functioning as an interrelated team with a common set of goals, information, and ground rules. This new approach is already common in many companies; in others, it is just emerging. It is only a matter of time before this formal, integrated computer-based system becomes commonplace in managing inventories as part of the overall approach to managing the total business.

The key to development and adoption of the new approach is the computer. Two developments brought about this revolution in how companies manage inventory and production. First are the dramatic changes in the cost/performance statistics of computers, as indicated by significant decreases in hardware costs. The second is the convergence of thinking in software development.

Example

A small electronics manufacturer produces a limited variety of surge suppressors for electrical systems. To control the materials ordering, the plant manager installed a Radio Shack TRS-80 microcomputer and supporting software programs. At the time of purchase the total cost of hardware and software was less than $1,500. The MRP software program cost $80. This system met the needs of this $1 million sales company for two years until a larger computer system was purchased.

Computer hardware and software advances have provided the means to have integrated information for complex inventory systems. Integrated information means that all company functions use the same database and records for their information needs and decision making. The computerized inventory purchasing example presented earlier is an example of using integrated information.

Database Files and Records

Integrated information depends on integrated databases. The term "database" refers to a whole set of related files and records. A record is a set of related pieces of data or information about something. The data in a record can be classified as primary data or secondary data. The secondary data describe something about the primary data and are used to relate files. Files are collections of records that have the same types of data that are arranged in the same physical format.

These concepts can be illustrated by returning to the inventory control and purchasing example. An inventory record and purchasing record are shown in Exhibit 5-2.

Exhibit 5-2
Inventory and Purchase Order Records

Part Number	Description	On Hand Quantity	On Order Quantity	ABC
101	Nut	100	500	A

Inventory Record

Purchase Order Number	Part Number Ordered	Quantity On Order	Vendor
1501	101	500	XYZ

Purchase Order Record

Each of these records consists of primary and secondary data. The primary datum for the inventory record is the part number. The description, quantity on hand, quantity on order and ABC classification are secondary data. The primary datum for the purchase order record is the purchase order number, and the secondary data are the part number, quantity on order, and the vendor(s).

The secondary data, in both cases, describe something about the primary data. Note that the quantity on order exists in both records as secondary data. There are two reasons for this. First, the quantity on order data are actually two different pieces of data. The quantity on order in the inventory record is the total on order for that part number. The quantity on order for the purchase order received is the quantity ordered on that single purchase order for that part number. There may be additional parts ordered on that purchase order number, in which case there would be multiple purchase records, or there may be additional purchase orders for the same part. The second reason for the same data existing in two records is for information processing speed and reference. The quantity on order for a part number can be found quickly by looking at that data field on the inventory record. Similarly, if there are multiple purchase orders for a part number and one is delayed for some reason, that purchase order quantity can be quickly identified from the purchase order record and used to adjust the inventory record data.

The inventory file would consist of all inventory records and the purchase order file would consist of all purchase order records. These files can be used to develop a database. The database may be expanded to include other files, such as the bill of materials.

Conceptually, records, files, and databases are the same in manual and computerized systems. However, the physical arrangement, the precision of that arrangement, and the processing logic are more exact in computer systems. This exactness is required because the computer is a rather stupid brute that relies on a set of instructions called a program, or software, to process the data from records, files, and databases. Because the computer is so fast in processing data, more integrated, accurate and detailed management of inventory can be achieved than is practical manually.

Information Pyramids

The value of the more detailed and accurate data depends on the kinds of decisions being made. The information needed for aggregate inventory management is different in form and detail from that needed for managing the inventory levels of individual items. With computerized systems, the higher-level management summary information can be based on integrated, accurate, and detailed information. This is not possible in manual systems because of the characteristics of manual systems shown earlier in Exhibit 5-1.

Exhibit 5-3
Planned Versus Actual Levels

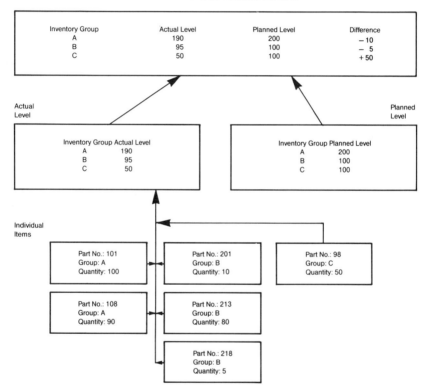

This concept of higher-level summaries, or information pyramids, may be illustrated with the example and data shown in Exhibit 5-3. The higher-level summaries are developed based on more detailed data collected at lower levels. In a similar manner, decisions and plans made at higher levels can be exploded downward to develop more detailed, accurate decisions and plans at lower levels. Actual results, such as production or inventory levels, may be compared with planned levels so that corrective actions may be taken. The impact of these corrective actions can rapidly and accurately be pictured throughout all levels of the information pyramid. Second generation closed-loop MRP systems (described in Chapter 4) are applications of this concept.

The number of levels in the inventory management information pyramid and the inventory files and records used at each level depend on the complexity and degree of integration of the inventory system. As the number of levels and number of files and records increase, the need for computerized inventory systems increases as well. In organizations where the number of inventory items is small and where there is little need to integrate the inventory decisions, manual systems may be used effectively to manage inventories. However, as discussed earlier, in today's (and tomorrow's) environment, inventory management is strategically important and, as such, inventory decisions must be part of the formal, integrated, overall management system of most firms. In addition, the economic tradeoff between manual and computerized systems is increasingly favoring computerized inventory management systems.

The concept of information pyramids leads to a consideration of the subsystems that comprise an inventory management system. In the following sections these subsystems are described and survey results are presented that summarize the extent to which computerization has occurred.

Inventory Management Information Systems

An integrated materials management information system would include the subsystems shown in Exhibit 5-4. It should be noted that these information subsystems exist in all inventory systems whether formal or informal, manual or computerized, or integrated or nonintegrated.

Forecasts of future demand for finished goods and merchandise are made by someone using some method. These forecasts, along with general ledger accounting records and the goals of the firm, are used to develop an overall business plan for sales and production. In a manufacturing environment, the overall production plan is translated into a master production schedule that identifies when and how much finished goods will be produced. The master production schedule (or sales plan, if not a manufacturing firm), the product structure bill of materials record, and the inventory status record are used to explode material (or distribution) requirements as described in Chapter 4. The material (or distribution) requirements and cost accounting records are used to make inventory management decisions (when and how much to order) and to develop production schedules.

Exhibit 5-4
Inventory Management Information Systems

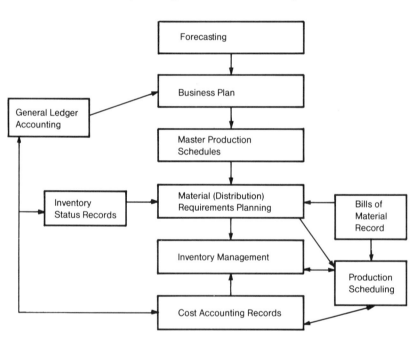

In computerized systems, each of these subsystems would have a set of files and records and a software program to process the data contained in those files and records. These software modules would provide the information needed for processing in other modules. For example, the MRP or DRP software would process the bill of materials data, inventory status data, and master production schedule to generate time-phased material requirements. This information would then serve as an input to the inventory management and production scheduling software to make decisions about when and how much to order. The information outputs of the various subsystems become data inputs to other subsystems. For subsystems such as the inventory status records — where the processing logic is easily programmable, computer software will provide faster and more accurate processing of data inputs into information outputs than manual systems. However, for subsystems where the processing logic is more judgmental or too complex to capture, as in developing the business plan, managerial intervention is required. In some subsystems, such as the master production schedule, a combination of software processing and managerial intervention may be used. The software may develop a first-cut master schedule that is then reviewed by management before being accepted as the data input for the material requirements explosion. Current research in expert systems and artificial intelligence promises to reduce the need for unnecessary, time-consuming managerial intervention.

In a fully integrated inventory management information system, software is needed not only to process the data within the subsystems but also to handle the information among subsystems. This requires a level of exactness in data, data processing logic, decision criteria, and decision rules that does not exist in many firms. This shortcoming may explain the lack of successful implementation of some closed-loop MRP systems reported in previous studies and confirmed in the survey results for this report.[2]

Software Selection

Computerization of the inventory management information system requires the selection of appropriate software. The software selection problem involves two interrelated decisions: first, a decision about the information processing requirements of the software and, second, a decision as to whether the software will be developed in-house or purchased from a vendor.

The information processing requirements of the software depend on the subsystems to be computerized, the desired degree of integration among the subsystems, and the complexity of the inventory system. Those subsystems that have a large number of records to be processed and have a well-defined processing logic are the most likely candidates for software programming. These subsystems must be sufficiently formalized before attempting to computerize them.

Once the subsystems to be computerized have been identified and their processing (software) needs have been determined, the next issue is the desired integration of the subsystems. For low degrees of integration, stand-alone software programs are acceptable. Unintegrated, stand-alone packages are easier to design and the cost is less than integrated software, since each system may have its own database or data specifications, and the database may be different for each system. Design specifications and the time required to program each module should be much less than if integration with other subsystems is required. The major disadvantage is that they are not integrated and each may require its own database. Over time, this approach may be difficult to maintain when multiple databases, not connected in any way, have to be updated on a regular basis.

At the other extreme is the totally integrated software approach where there is only one database and an overall processing logic tying all subsystems together. The major advantage is that one database serves the needs of many users, and one update is all that is required. The major disadvantage is the cost involved in the design of such a system since common features of all decision areas have to be specified and considered, as well as the unique needs or features of any one decision area. A commitment to this type of system usually requires substantial resources in order for the project to be successful.

An intermediate approach is a modular design where subsystems software can be operated independently or integrated with other subsystems software. Modular software offers the possibility of moving toward integration. However, this flexibility is traded for reduced individual subsystem flexibility. Modular software programming design costs would be more expensive than standalone software. The major advantage is the ability to move toward full integration in a piecemeal fashion.

Once the software integration approach has been determined, a company faces a make-or-buy decision. The make approach is to design and program the software within the company, so that the software can be customized to meet the needs of the company. Developing software in-house allows a company to design the software to fit its specific needs. The major disadvantages are that the company may not have sufficient programming staff or may be reinventing the wheel.

Buying software from vendors has the advantage of a shorter development time and possibly lower costs. The specifications for the database are known, and the types and formats of reports established. To get such a system up and running, a company needs to convert data into a predetermined format and input this into the system. Usually, this type of system may be installed and running much quicker than one where the software is designed in-house. Thus, management is buying time by purchasing the software from outside vendors.

Another advantage is the expertise purchased with the software. Many companies do not have the staff to design and program such systems; thus, the only alternative is to purchase outside. When outside vendors are used, the expertise may be based on the installation of similar systems in various companies with many of the same types of inventory items and problems. Therefore, many of the potential problems may have been recognized and provided for in the purchasing system.

The major disadvantage of purchasing a system is the nature of the design of the system. Each company has some unique features and purchased systems frequently do not satisfy all these needs. Management then has to learn to operate with a system that, while adequate, provides less than optimum output for its particular firm.

Example

The software programmer of a software design firm once said that two of the three biggest lies in this industry are: "it's a turnkey system" and "the programs are completely integratable". Very few companies are able to purchase business application software that does not require substantial customization.

Survey Results

Application Areas

Overall, over 77% of the respondents to the survey indicated that their firm used a computer-based inventory management system. While this is a large percentage, it is surprising that virtually all were not using a computer-based management system for at least one of the subsystems indicated in Exhibit 5-4. The percentage of response of use by subsystem is shown in Exhibit 5-5.

Exhibit 5-5
Types of Software Applications

Type of Application	Percentage of Companies Indicating Use
General ledger accounting	75.3%
Cost accounting	67.1
Inventory management	56.2
Bill of materials	54.8
Material requirements planning	47.9
Production scheduling and control	45.2
Master scheduling	42.5
Forecasting	37.0
Other	5.5

An examination of Exhibit 5-5 indicates that there are few companies applying software in areas not listed above. The percentage of other uses is only about 5%, which would indicate the most common computer applications are included in the list.

Almost all of the areas included in the list are popular with the companies responding to the questionnaire. The most common, general ledger accounting, should surprise no one. Accounting systems were among the first wide-scale commercial applications of computers. These survey results indicate that computers are used most frequently for those subsystems characterized by large data processing requirements and by straightforward, easy to program logic. One would expect master scheduling to be one of the least frequent applications because this subsystem and its underlying decision-making logic have yet to be formalized in many firms. What is surprising from these results is the relatively low usage of computer-based forecasting. While numerous computer forecasting programs are available, the low percentage of use of such systems may indicate that in most firms this subsystem—like master scheduling—has yet to be formalized.

Inventory management is the third most frequently cited use of computers and may be further divided as shown in Exhibit 5-6. The transaction history percentage indicates that computers are used most frequently in the inventory management information functions of data entry, record keeping, and data processing. Similarly, purchase order preparation, order calculation, cycle counting, and ABC analysis percentages indicate that computers are less frequently used in activities related to inventory report generation and decision making. This is not surprising since a high degree of accuracy must be achieved in the data entry, record keeping and data processing functions before computers can be used effectively in decision making and report generation. One would expect that these percentages would increase over time as firms improve their record-keeping accuracy.

Exhibit 5-6
Computer Applications in Inventory Management Subsystems

Subsystem Applications	Percentage of Companies Indicating Use
Transaction history	80.8%
Vendor identification	61.6
Multi-locations	57.5
Purchase order preparation	52.1
Order calculation	47.9
Cycle counting	45.2
ABC analysis	45.2

Software Characteristics

Exhibit 5-7 presents the survey results concerning the nature of the software package applications listed in Exhibit 5-5. These statistics indicate that almost half of the companies have computer software that can stand alone or be integrated for most decision areas. This may indicate that some of the subsystems are still under development, and the modules are designed in such a way that integration is possible only for those subsystems where such integration is desirable. This may include such subsystems as inventory management and production scheduling, as well as general ledger and cost accounting. There may or may not be a need to integrate subsystems, such as forecasting and general ledger accounting, unless there is another subsystem, such as production scheduling, that is integrated with each of the other subsystems. Using stand-alone modules provides the greatest flexibility for a company at a minimum cost as long as the various modules have the ability to be integrated. This would suggest that one database can serve most of these needs.

Exhibit 5-8 represents the survey results concerning the source of these software packages. These results indicate a preference for in-house design for all subsystem applications surveyed. This is true in all cases except for the "other" category where the results are almost even. As an area becomes more unique to a company, it becomes

Exhibit 5-7
Design Characteristics of Software Packages

Software Type	Percentage Using This Type of Software
Unintegrated, standalone packages for most decision areas	28.8%
Modules that can standalone or be integrated for most decision areas	43.8
Most decision areas totally integrated into single or separate packages	26.0
Not applicable	2.4
Total	100.0%

more difficult to purchase software off the shelf, and the frequency of companies designing software in-house increases significantly. This is supported by the high frequency of companies designing their own software in the area of production scheduling. If any area is different among and between companies, production scheduling would probably be it. This problem should not be as difficult to overcome in the areas of inventory management and general ledger accounting, since many of the procedures and techniques of these subsystems have been formalized and standardized from one company to the other. These are areas where many companies can and do purchase their software.

In looking at the percentages, software is designed in-house almost two-thirds of the time. Companies would seem to be designing their inventory management systems to fit the particular needs of their company and incorporating specific decision parameters into such programs.

Software packages have been available from outside vendors since the early 1970s.[3] As indicated in Chapter 4, MRP systems have been commercially available since about 1971.[4] Most of the commercially available software seems to be of the type that permits modules to stand alone but also allows them to be integrated as the company wishes. This provides the greatest flexibility in the installation of such a system as a company may install one or two or as many modules as desired. Most of these packages have a cost accounting module, although not usually a rigorous standard cost accounting system. They might have a manufacturing requirements planning module(s), a general ledger module, a production scheduling module and, perhaps, a forecasting module. An inventory management and control module may be incorporated into the cost accounting module or be a standalone unit. These systems are available for mainframe computers, minicomputers and, more recently, for applications with a microcomputer having a hard disk. It is reasonable to expect that, in the near future, a computerized inventory management system will be available for any company that has a microcomputer system. This would include most companies, except for those very small ones that usually would not have an inventory management information system problem because of the size of inventory.

Exhibit 5-8
Sources of Software Applications

Subsystem Software Application	In-house	Purchased Outside
General ledger accounting	55.3%	44.7%
Cost accounting	79.1	20.9
Inventory management	67.5	32.5
Bill of materials	70.0	30.0
Materials requirements planning	60.0	40.0
Production scheduling and control	79.4	20.6
Master scheduling	70.9	29.1
Forecasting	81.4	18.2
Other	50.0	50.0

Summary

Inventory management information systems serve three functions. They are: 1) inventory data entry and record keeping, 2) inventory data processing, and 3) inventory decision making and report generation. Historically, these systems have been manual, informal systems. Computer-related technology advances in performance and costs and increased market competition have forced most companies to computerize some, if not most, of their inventory management information systems. Survey results indicate that the subsystems of this information system that are most frequently computerized include bill of materials, materials requirement planning, master scheduling, cost accounting, general ledger accounting, and transaction history. Software programs for these subsystems most frequently are designed in-house on a modular basis for future integration.

Notes

[1] For a more detailed discussion of these concepts, the reader should see Dees, Paul, *Production and Inventory Management in the Technological Age*, Prentice-Hall, Inc., 1983.

[2] Anderson, John C., Roger S. Schroeder, Sharon E. Tupy and Edna M. White, "Material Requirements Planning: The State of the Art," *Production and Inventory Management*, Vol. 23, No. 4, Fourth Quarter 1983, pp. 51-67.

[3] One of the earliest and most popular computerized inventory systems was COPICS (Communications Oriented Production Information and Control System). This was developed and sold by IBM, and materials describing such a program have a March 1972 date. More sophisticated and advanced systems are now available.

[4] A computerized inventory system for manufacturing (MRP) was illustrated in a paper presented at the annual APICS conference held in 1971 in Cincinnati, Ohio. See Chapter 4 for a more complete description of this system.

Chapter 6

Measuring Inventory Management Effectiveness

After an inventory management and control system is installed and operating, a company should monitor such a system for two reasons. One is related to the control or accuracy of the records while the other is concerned with the amount of investment in inventory. Since it is usually not feasible to monitor all items in an inventory system, some technique should be employed that would allow a firm to monitor those items that are material in nature or have a large annual usage. One such technique is the ABC system.

ABC Classification of Inventory Items

Efforts to set inventory policy at the executive level in an organization, even though the policy is carried out at the operating level, are greatly aided by a characteristic of inventory that seems to be almost universal: a few items in inventory account for much of the value during a time period. This relationship is usually such that about 20% of the number of items account for about 80% of the value. It is sometimes called Pareto's Law. Exhibit 6-1 is an example of such a relationship.

The data from Exhibit 6-1 are shown in graph form as Exhibit 6-2. This relationship holds true for other inventory related relationships, i.e.:

1. A few of the customers provide most of the profit dollars.
2. A few items in the inventory provide most of the profit dollars.
3. A few inventory items account for most of the stockouts.
4. A few vendors are responsible for most of the problems with purchase items.

Exhibit 6-1
Example of the ABC Classification

Percentage of items	Number of items	Dollar value of usage	Percentage of total value
5%	141	$4,729,573.11	64.48%
12	283	5,677,909.09	77.41
17	424	6,194,850.48	84.46
23	565	6,534,328.28	89.09
29	706	6,778,398.81	92.41
35	848	6.948,536.90	94.73
40	989	7,065,526.39	96.33
46	1,130	7,149,083.01	97.47
52	1,271	7,208,652,52	98.28
58	1,413	7,252,632.28	98.88
64	1,554	7,282,300.36	99.30
69	1,695	7,305,277.45	99.60
75	1,836	7,319,164.98	99.79
81	1,978	7,327,231.42	99.90
87	2,119	7,331,846.58	99.96
92	2,260	7,334,056.92	99.99
98	2,401	7,334,808.23	100.00
100	2,448	7,334,842.67	100.00

It is possible to expand the ABC classification and take, for example, the A items and separate these into A, B, C categories. Using this approach, the table in Exhibit 6-3 on page 106 may be prepared.

This exhibit was prepared by multiplying the previous number by 20% for the percent and number of items and by 80% for the dollar value. This follows the general rule of thumb that 20% of the items account for 80% of the value. In the example above, after two iterations, 4% of the inventory items account for $640,000, or 64% of the inventory value.

Using the ABC classification, different inventory policies may be established for various groups, with the costs of such policies matched against the benefits to be realized. For example, a two-bin method could be used with C items, the EOQ technique applied to the B items, and a fixed period review approach used with A items. The criterion is that of cost/benefit, with the benefits of the inventory systems being larger than the costs of installing and using such a system. Or, the classification may be used in a modular approach to

Exhibit 6-2
Graphical Illustration of ABC Classification

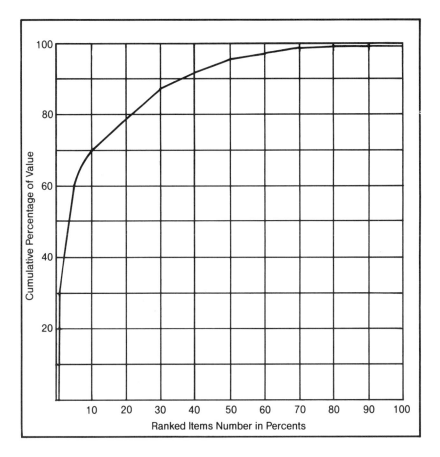

installing an inventory system with the A items receiving attention first, then the B items, and, if the cost/benefit is there, using a formalized system for the C items. The point is to match the requirements to the underlying inventory that has the greatest usage value.

Once inventory items have been selected for evaluation or inventory policies have been determined for chosen groups of inventories, it is necessary to monitor these policies in order to determine levels of compliance or accuracy of records. A common procedure for doing this is cycle counting.

Exhibit 6-3
Illustration of ABC Classification
Inventory with 10,000 Items

% of items in group	No. of items	$ value	Class
100%	10,000	$1,000,000	ABC
20	2,000	800,000	A
4	800	640,000	AA

Cycle Counting

Cycle counting involves sampling groups of inventory at regular intervals of time and verifying the count and quantity of the items. Pertinent inventory policies may also be tested to ensure compliance with these policies. This is particularly important if unplanned stockouts are occurring or if other inventory problems have developed. Cycle counting avoids a costly shutdown of a facility for an annual physical count, which, in most cases, is not timely in recognizing inventory problems. In order for an inventory system to function properly, such a system must be monitored constantly. Cycle counting does this. In addition, inventory counting can be handled by stockroom personnel during off-peak hours, with these few employees trained to be far more accurate counters than personnel who only take inventory once a year.

Cycle counting of inventories includes three phases: Phase I is designed to identify and eliminate errors; Phase II is intended to verify the high level of inventory accuracy to the satisfaction of management and auditors; and Phase III is intended to measure continuing accuracy levels and adherence to management inventory policies.

Any system, because of the human element as well as other factors, will generate errors in inventory records. Cycle counting should identify these errors. Counts are made and compared with records, and adjustments are made to the records where necessary.

For financial reporting and for management use, it is necessary to have reasonably accurate inventory records. While financial reporting requires a high degree of accuracy, the needs of inventory information users require some degree of consistency in the records. Otherwise, problems develop with established management policies, or in the worst case situation misleading financial statements are issued.

Continuing accuracy levels and adherence to management policies may only be achieved with frequent monitoring of the inventory system. Where frequent monitoring does not exist, systems have a tendency to degenerate within a relatively short period of time.

All of the benefits from cycle counting are not without costs. There are obvious disadvantages to such a technique. The problem of establishing paperwork cutoff dates is difficult enough for an annual physical inventory, but becomes extremely challenging for counts made while normal activity is going on. Picking up the paperwork in the system so that the inventory can be reconciled properly to the records requires considerable ingenuity and discipline. The most serious disadvantage of the cycle-count system is that it is often done by personnel who normally have sufficient time to handle it. When activity picks up, however, there is always great reluctance to add more personnel. In order to permit personnel to handle other duties during periods of heavy activity, cycle counting is too often temporarily discontinued.

Annual physical inventories or cycle counts are not a substitute for good records and discipline in handling paperwork. Many companies recognize their failure to maintain accurate records, but they often depend solely on the physical inventories to straighten out the records. Unless the failures that caused the records to go wrong are corrected, the records will always be in error and shortages and overstocking problems will continue to exist.

Example

Firm XYZ had a recurring problem of controlling component inventory items. The physical count was rarely in agreement with the record count. The result and/or cause of this was that the production scheduler would go to the stockroom and stage parts for withdrawal to support the MRP schedule before the parts were actually needed. In addition, these parts were ordered as replacement parts by field distribution. These orders were typically placed before they were needed because of past difficulties in receiving orders when needed.

An ABC analysis was performed to identify the "A" items, or the 20% of the items causing 80% of the inaccuracies. Once identified, these items were locked up in closed stores and cycle counted frequently. After these changes, inventory record accuracy improved to the point where less frequent physical counts were needed.

Once an inventory system is under control, management needs to direct its attention to managing the inventory as suggested in the previous chapters. To evaluate how well such a system is performing, there are several tools and techniques available to measure efficiency and effectiveness. The traditional techniques used for monitoring inventory performance may be stated in either nondollar or dollar amounts. Each group of techniques provides different types of information.

Nondollar Measures

Ratios are one of the most common techniques for measuring inventory performance.

Turnover Ratios

Turnover ratios appear to be the most popular type of performance measure for inventory management policies. Turnover is the number of times a base, or denominator, can be divided into a numerator. While the number of potential turnover ratios, using accounting data, is almost endless since each number could be divided into any other number, some of the most common ways in which inventory turnovers are computed are as follows:

1. All inventories $= \dfrac{\text{Cost of goods sold}}{\text{Average total inventories}}$

2. Finished goods $= \dfrac{\text{Cost of goods sold}}{\text{Average finished goods inventories}}$

3. Work-in-process $= \dfrac{\text{Cost of goods manufactured}}{\text{Average inventory of work in process}}$

4. Raw materials $= \dfrac{\text{Cost of materials used}}{\text{Average raw materials inventory}}$

Because these figures are derived from accounting data, they are influenced by the accounting methods designed for measuring periodic income. Thus, a writedown of inventory will usually be charged against cost of goods sold so that the writedown, which may be an indicator of inventory inefficiency, will increase the inventory turnover. In the case of a writedown, both the numerator and denominator are changed with the numerator — cost of goods sold — being increased and the denominator — average inventories — being decreased. Thus, the effect on the turnover ratios is twofold, and a small writedown may cause a significant change in the underlying ratio.

Furthermore, the variety of inventory costing methods now in use make the interpretation of an inventory turnover figure extremely complex. How, if at all, is one to interpret the ratio of the current cost of goods sold to the average inventory costed by the last-in first-out (LIFO) method. The LIFO inventory is costed at prices current many years ago. Apart from costing problems, attempts to determine the turnover are beset by various other problems of aggregation. For instance, a moderately rapid turnover ratio for the inventory may obscure the fact that half of the inventory is turning very slowly and the other half very rapidly.

Using Turnover Ratios

Turnover computations are more meaningful and more useful if computed on a unit basis so that problems of aggregation are minimized. For an individual stockkeeping item, turnover may be the ratio of the number of units issued to the average number of units on hand. Note that using absolute values, such as units, eliminates the accounting problems of inventory costing. However, such a method does present a problem since calculating ratios on a unit basis is much more time consuming than using an aggregate inventory value, which is readily available from the underlying accounting records.

In some applications, it may be more meaningful to compare current inventory against parameters such as order points, safety stocks, etc., rather than months of inventory. This method of evaluation is easy to program and is very helpful if a fully automated system is not available to help monitor inventory and priorities.

Limits of Analysis Using Turnover Ratios

Even on a unit by unit or subunit basis, the information provided by a turnover ratio is questionable. Compare the turnover ratio with the concepts of the fixed or variable period inventory systems discussed previously. Turnover is a minimum concept, whereas the two inventory management models presented in this study provide optimum concepts. According to one traditional use of turnover, the higher the turnover, the lower the inventory in relation to cost of goods sold, the better the system of inventory management and control. However, an infinite turnover can be achieved by carrying no inventory whatsoever. Such an inventory procedure would not be a good policy because a company with no inventory would be continuously buying, expediting, and apologizing for slow deliveries. Any meaningful application of the turnover concept must, therefore, contain the implicit assumption that high turnover is only desirable to the extent that it is compatible with efficient operations. Turnover is worth improving only if there is no substantial increase in ordering cost or significant loss of sales resulting from excessive stockouts. The turnover ratio is only useful if it can be related in some way to the costs of inventory management and the optimum decisions of when and how much to order.

It may be that the role for the turnover computation is in determining if the inventory investment is in substantial agreement with management policies. Management may use the turnover ratio to judge whether the inventory system is, in fact, operating in accordance with specifications. Thus, it might be possible to take a small sample of inventory items, and, for each of these items, compute both the inventory implied by the selected inventory policies and for the actual turnover experienced. If an excessive proportion of the actual turnovers deviate from the implied turnovers, the inventory manager may conclude that further investigation is necessary to see whether the system policies and procedures are being followed. A ratio may best serve management in the role of highlighting exceptions rather than measuring efficiency and effectiveness.

Management may wish to use individual inventory records rather than aggregate ones. In many cases this may lead to a more rational evaluation of the underlying inventory problems or a more accurate evaluation of the relationship of inventories on hand to sales and production goals.

Example

The data for a firm's inventory turnover ratios are given in Exhibit 6-4. Listed are ten inventory items, with an average usage of ten units per month. While the current inventory records show that overall there are two months of inventory on hand (100 units x two months), closer inspection indicates that four of the items have less than one month of inventory (A, D, E, and F), and five items have less than two months (A, D, E, F, and J). Although the controller may be very satisfied with the overall investment in inventory, the marketing or production areas have to be concerned about continuing sales and/or production. To arrive at the available inventory for one month, the current inventory is compared against one month's usage and the current level of inventory or one month's usage, whichever is smaller, is considered available. By totaling the available inventories, there are 74 units or 74% available inventory at the one-month level. The same process can be done at the two-month level, where there is a 58% available inventory.

Exhibit 6-4
Turnover Calculation of Individual Units

Item	One month usage	Current inventory	One month available inventory	Two months' available inventory
A	10	7	7	7
B	12	38	12	24
C	13	40	13	26
D	8	3	3	3
E	14	1	1	1
F	11	0	0	0
G	6	18	12	12
H	9	39	9	18
I	7	43	7	14
J	10	11	10	11
Total	100	200	74	116

74 / 100 = 74% available inventory for one-month level.
116 / 200 = 58% available inventory for two-month level.

Percent of Late Orders

Late orders are those that are received or shipped beyond the desired or quoted due date or lead time. Probably the second most commonly used ratio of inventory and operating performance is the percent of orders that are late. This ratio may be used to measure customer or supplier service. As a result, it is usually calculated for individual finished goods or raw material orders. For this measure, the desired performance level is always zero. Incoming or outgoing orders should never be late. If they are, then the desired or planned lead time is inaccurate, or there has been some kind of interruption in the system.

Stockout (Backorders) Frequencies or Percentages

Stockouts are items that are not in inventory when they are needed. Stockouts may result in backorders or lost sales for finished goods. Work-in-process and raw material stockouts typically are backordered or expedited. The number of stockouts, in an absolute sense or as a percent of total orders, is an important measure of customer service for finished goods and of operating efficiency for work-in-process and raw materials. Various definitions of stockouts may be used, with those most commonly used being described in the customer service discussion presented in Chapter 2.

Lead Time

Another popular performance measure is that of monitoring lead times. These may be expressed as a percentage of some base, as absolute numbers, or as variations from normal. These are applied most often for raw materials and finished goods and almost always on an individual item basis.

As was noted earlier, the gross turnover ratios may not be sensitive enough to effectively monitor inventory performance on a regular basis. Such is not the case where lead times are used as a standard. Changes from these standards may be tracked by key inventory items and adjustments made where needed in either follow-ups with vendors or by selecting alternative sources of supply. By planning and controlling lead times, stockouts, and excessive safety stock, late orders can be reduced.

Number of Orders or Setups

Where this method is applied, it is used most often in monitoring performance for work-in-process. Planning orders, setups, or shop loads and scheduling these activities are two sides of the same coin. Planning the number of orders seems to be one of the more feasible ways of planning, controlling, and evaluating work-in-process inventory. Establishing a standard or expected number of orders allows management to plan usage of available capacity, while comparing the planned number with the actual number of orders permits management to control and to evaluate plant utilization.

Dollar Measures

Rather than nondollar measures, some companies may prefer to use dollar measures of inventory effectiveness. It is possible to compute a dollar amount for an optimum level of inventory, and then compare this optimum level with the actual dollar level. In other words, it is possible to determine what the inventory dollar level should be in accordance with the inventory management system policies, and then compare the actual inventory dollars with the theoretical amount.

In making this computation, the inventory consists not only of the stock on hand but also the items on order and is divided into three categories:

1. Those items where the quantity on hand and on order is below the minimum desired level (safety stock).
2. Those items where the quantity on hand and on order is above the maximum desired level (safety stock plus EOQ or average order).
3. Those items between the minimum and maximum desired level.

Applying the lower of cost or market concept, the desired inventory investment can be calculated as follows. The data are assumed to have been taken from audited inventory prices and quantities or may be done on a sampling basis using perpetual inventory records, if there is reasonable confidence in the underlying accuracy of the inventory records and prices.

1. a. Dollar value of inventory of items below the minimum desired level (safety stock) $211,000

   b. Dollar investment necessary to bring inventory items up to minimum desired level   17,000

2. a. Dollar amount of inventory items above the maximum desired level (safety stock plus EOQ or average order)   83,000

b. Subtract dollar amount of investment of
    inventory above the maximum desired
    level   (9,000)
3. Dollar amount inventory items between
    the minimum and maximum desired levels   9,822,000
    Total acceptable inventory investment $10,124,000

This calculation is shown in graphic form in Exhibit 6-5.

Exhibit 6-5
Calculation of Total Acceptable Inventory Investment

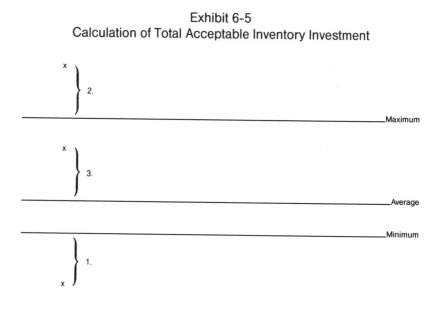

The closer the actual inventory is to this acceptable inventory
investment, the better the system is operating in accordance with
specifications. If the ratio of actual inventory to the acceptable
inventory investment is close to one, then the system is operating in
control. The further the ratio departs from one, the stronger the
evidence that the system is not operating according to established
management policies.

This calculation also provides some estimate of the potential savings
from changing the inventory system. This computation is shown in
Exhibit 6-6.

Exhibit 6-6
Calculation of Potential Savings

Actual inventory investment in dollars	$18,000,000
Optimum level of inventory investment in dollars	10,124,000
Potential savings from inventory system	$ 7,876,000

Frequency of Monitoring

Using a technique such as the one described above, one may monitor how well the inventory system is operating and/or the potential savings from the installation of such a system. Because of the calculations involved, the application of such procedures should be done on a rather infrequent basis, or when changes to the current operating system are to be considered. Obviously, the cost/benefit is such that frequent calculations are not reasonable. This is not true where ratios are used. Where ratios are applied as a measure of inventory performance, monthly or quarterly monitoring is feasible, since the cost of calculation of the ratios is small and it is important to highlight trends as soon as possible. Integration of techniques, such as ratios with dollar amounts, allows a company to use both short-run and long-run monitoring devices. Ratios may be considered the short-run and dollar amounts the long-run techniques available.

Performance Standards

The essence of inventory management is making decisions of when and how much to order to bring actual inventory levels within desired levels. The previous discussions on various measures of inventory performance have alluded to performance standards. Performance standards may be developed based on past performance, industry performance, or planned performance derived from operations and inventory strategies.

Historical and past-experience-derived standards are typically found in organizations where inventory management is not a strategic nor a competitive concern. Most often, these organizations compete based on some competence other than cost or at least cost is a relatively low priority criterion vis-à-vis quality or customer service. As firms experience increased competition, industry performance standards are adopted. Inventory management is still not a strategic concern, but it is important to remain competitive in the marketplace. Industry inventory management practices are likely to become more important.

As competition becomes more intense and cost becomes increasingly important, firms will adopt performance standards for operations and inventories based on systematic planning and management. Thus, optimum levels of inventory, lead times, stockouts, and so on are derived based on inventory management systems linked to the strategy of the organization.

Example

General Electric and IBM[1] adopted manufacturing excellence strategies for their strategic business units in the early 1980's. In each case, product cost, quality level, lead time, inventory turnover and other performance standards were adopted as goals to increase their competitiveness in the marketplace. Product design, marketing, and production developed standards to measure how well the strategy was achieved. For GE dishwashers, one of the standards was a goal of 25 inventory turns by 1983 and 28 turns by 1984. Both these standards were far in excess of what the GE dishwasher had historically achieved and, in excess of industry standards.

Standards based on past experience or industry performance are usually driven by financial statement reporting concerns instead of "optimal" operating performance concerns. Inventories fluctuate to meet the financial statement performance needs at quarter-end and/or year-end. This often results in what George W. Plossl has called the "INSANE cycle".[2] The acronym stands for inventory service and net earnings, and it applies to those cases where operations and inventories fluctuate alternately between meeting customer needs and showing financial profits. This oversimplified approach to establishing inventory performance standards is not consistent with the management approaches presented in this text, but it is undoubtedly used in many organizations today.

Survey Results

Ninety-five percent of the companies responding to the questionnaire stated that inventory performance is monitored. Surprisingly, only 44% of the respondents indicated that ABC analysis is used. This may be because many firms have computerized their systems, allowing all inventory items to be systematically managed and, thereby, obviating the need for ABC analysis. Over 60% of the respondents indicated that they cycle count inventories, with raw materials and finished goods being the items most frequently cycle counted.

Performance Measures Used

Virtually all of the performance measures discussed in this chapter are used to measure inventory management effectiveness, with turnover ratios being the most popular. This is true regardless of the type of inventory involved. Data from the questionnaire also indicate that turnover ratios are applied to total inventories much more frequently than to individual items within an inventory. This would suggest that turnover ratios are being used to measure a particular company's ratios against an industry average or standard applied to gross inventories. One of the reasons for the popularity of such gross data is the ease with which such industry data may be obtained, since it may be estimated from typical financial statements or obtained from various industry and governmental publications. There is a strong probability that the profits of some companies could be improved if the focus of attention on inventory management were shifted from turnover ratios to some of the other techniques discussed in this chapter. The turnover ratios for a particular company may be within limits prescribed by management or an industry, and, yet, the inventory may be at an excessive level.

A large percentage of the companies responding to the questionnaire used dollar amounts to measure obsolete inventory. This is true across all types of inventories, with more than 30% of the companies using such a technique. The questionnaire was not designed to solicit responses on such questions as what is obsolete inventory, how is it treated, the problems encountered, and related topics. These issues are beyond the scope of this study. When obsolete inventories are involved, the accounting for such obsolete inventory should consider the IRS position on deductibility of excess or obsolete inventory.[3]

Few firms used percentage of late orders for raw material or work-in-process inventories, but 27% indicated they used such a performance standard for finished goods. For those companies using ratios as a performance standard, this was the second most popular technique — turnover being the most popular. However, nonmanufacturing firms participating in the study relied almost exclusively on turnover ratios. Few of the other firms used anything else.

About one-quarter of the firms in the survey used a ratio of stockouts or backorders to finished goods performance measure. Few, if any, used any stockout measures for any other type of inventory. These results are consistent with those related to the location of safety stock. Over 60% of the firms maintain safety stock in finished goods with much smaller percentages holding safety stock in other inventories. It seems reasonable that a firm maintaining safety stock in the form of finished goods would monitor the stockouts or backorders in finished goods.

Surprisingly, lead time performance measures are one of the least used standards for the responding firms. This is true for both manufacturing and nonmanufacturing firms. Where lead time standards are used, they are used primarily for finished goods.

The number of orders or setups is the least frequently used standard for the responding firms. Where applied, it was almost entirely used to monitor work-in-process orders or setups. Almost none of the companies in the study used this technique for raw materials, or service parts, or other types of inventories, such as those found in retail firms.

Users of Inventory Performance Measures

Based upon the data from the questionnaire, the two major users of the inventory performance measures are accounting and top management; although other areas of a company, such as production planners, may also be users. One may suppose that performance measures are used in the variance analysis system to explain why variances occurred or to highlight potential corrective action that may be needed. With typical inventory carrying costs of 30% to 40%, attention by accounting and top management to the level of inventory and to the efficiency and effectiveness of the inventory management system provides a valuable source of profit dollars.

Frequency of Monitoring

The most common time period for calculation of ratios, as applied by the companies responding to the questionnaire, was monthly. A few companies used indicators on a weekly basis, but the majority used the month as the common time frame over which they compared actual inventory performance with some standard. This is a common time frame used in the accounting reports and, since the inventory measures were also calculated using accounting data such as cost of goods sold, it is not surprising that the same time frames are used for comparing standards against actual. Since most inventory items, when compared in total, are not unusually volatile, a time frame of one month should be sufficient to highlight trends that are developing and would be adequate for the lead time necessary for adjustments to become effective.

Performance Standards

Over 90% of the companies responding to the questionnaire indicated that experience is used to derive the performance standards. The survey did not provide data for determining how experience was used in arriving at such a performance standard. When asked this question in telephone interviews, the respondents indicated that the numbers were based on previous history of the company and on management beliefs of what the standards should be. Over 24% of the respondents indicated that integrated business and inventory planning are used, and over 65% indicated that forecasted inventory needs are used to derive performance standards.

With the popularity of microcomputers and the availability of software, such as spreadsheet programs, companies are increasingly able to get better control over their inventory systems, with little additional cost. This is one area of inventory management and control that could provide a substantial payoff for those companies where excessive inventories existed in prior periods. In this new environment, past history may provide little relevance for the levels of inventory that should occur in the future. Methods other than experience may be more appropriate in determining inventory standards of performance.

Summary

Management must be concerned with control as well as the effective and efficient use of the investment in inventory. This chapter describes two techniques for identifying and controlling inventory items. Cycle counting and ABC analysis may be employed where it is not feasible to look at each item in the inventory because of the cost involved in such a task. They allow management to focus on those items where the potential for large savings in inventory costs exists.

Two methods of evaluating existing inventory systems are also illustrated. One method relies on ratios while the other calculates dollar amounts.

Based upon an analysis of responses to the questionnaire used in the study, turnover ratios are the most popular method of performance measurement while calculation of obsolete inventory is the second most popular tool. Each compares actual data with standards derived primarily from past experience.

Notes

[1]Wheelwright, Steven C. and Robert H. Hayes, "Competing Through Manufacturing," *Harvard Business Review,* January-February 1985, pp. 99-109.

[2]For a more detailed discussion of these concepts, the reader should see George W. Plossl, *Manufacturing Control,* New York: Reston Publishing Company, 1973.

[3]*Thor Power Tool Co. vs IRS Commissioner,* 439 U.S. 522 (1979).

Chapter 7

Zero Inventories Approach to Inventory Management

During the last 23 years, since the 1964 NAA Research Study on Techniques in Inventory Management and Control, the competitive environment and prescribed management practices have changed dramatically. Of all the foreign (and now domestic) competitors, Japanese firms have been the most successful in avoiding noncompetitive production costs and poor quality.[1] While the reasons for success in today's competitive market are multifaceted, a corporate culture characterized by the pursuit of excellence in all aspects of the organization seems to be a common denominator of successful firms.[2]

The increasing penetration of Japanese manufacturers in selected U.S. markets has received widespread attention. In high-volume, repetitive manufactured product markets, the Japanese have produced remarkable results in inventory turnover, labor costs, quality, and capacity utilization. Because of these achievements, considerable attention has been focused on the way Japanese manufacturing firms are managed in general and, more specifically, how production and inventories are managed. A new approach to production and inventory management, called Zero Inventories (ZI) and/or Just-In-Time (JIT), has emerged in the 1980's as a way of improving manufacturing and distribution competitiveness. In this chapter, an overview of JIT/ZI is presented, the organizational and operational prerequisites of achieving such an approach are described, and case histories of successful implementations are reviewed.

Overview of Zero Inventories Approach

Zero Inventories and Just-In-Time production concepts are stockless production approaches. These approaches are changing the way managers view the role of production and inventory management in the total system; and they are affecting the way materials managers view the when and how much inventory management decisions. JIT/ZI systems represent the third generation of inventory management and control concepts.

The first generation of inventory management concepts occurred in the 1950's and 1960's and emphasized quantitative and statistically based techniques for independent demand. The Economic Order Quantity (EOQ) concept was the hallmark of this time. Material presented in Chapters 2 and 3 is representative of this "classical" approach to inventory management and was the state of the art at the time the 1964 NAA report on inventory management was published.

In the 1970's, MRP, the system of choice for many manufacturing companies, emphasized the computerized data and information processing systems approach to the management of dependent demand inventories. Such a system uses time phasing and net material requirements to manage dependent demand items. The material presented in Chapter 4 describes this approach and represents the state of the art in most organizations at the time this current report is being written.

The JIT/ZI approach differs from previous inventory management approaches in several respects. First, it is a change in the way managers think about and understand inventory management. It is more a philosophy than a system of management techniques. In JIT/ZI, inventory is viewed as a sign of waste and something that covers up other problems, such as long lead times or poor quality. In the first two generations of inventory approaches, the implicit assumption is that inventories act as the shock absorbers or buffers that are necessary for all rational and economic operations. The inventory management problem is to achieve the optimum level of inventory by deciding when and how much to order to minimize total inventory costs. The JIT/ZI approach is to find practical ways to eliminate the needs for inventories. The optimum level of inventories is zero and inventory should be ordered such that only the right material is in the right place at the right time. Reaching the ideal, or optimal, level of zero may not be literally possible, but that is not the point. The point is that the ideal of inventory elimination, and the degree to which it is achieved, is a measure of a firm's success in establishing a competitive edge in today's market.

Second, the JIT/ZI approach does not prescribe techniques or methodologies but, instead, prescribes an ideal or goal and practical ways to pursue that goal. Previous inventory methods focused on devising quantitative, statistical, and/or computer based technique-oriented solution methodologies. The material in Chapters 2, 3, and 4 reflects this technique orientation. JIT/ZI focuses upon finding ways to simplify and eliminate the problems that cause inventories, as opposed to finding optimal inventory level solutions for complex problems.

Third, the JIT/ZI approach focuses on the integrative nature of operational decisions. JIT/ZI involves every function in the organization and a total system, company-wide effort is needed. Finding practical ways to reduce the need for inventories may involve changes in departments as illustrated below.

	Department		Changes
1.	Marketing-Sales	a.	Eliminate inactive products
		b.	Develop reliable forecasts
2.	Engineering	a.	Standardize product design
		b.	Low-cost, high-quality design
		c.	Minimum of engineering changes
3.	Manufacturing/ Engineering	a.	Reduction of setup times
		b.	Improved plant layout for process flow
		c.	Automated production with robotics, CNC, etc.
4.	Quality Assurance	a.	Zero defects programs
		b.	Vendor quality assurance program
		c.	Process control
5.	Human Resources	a.	Education and training programs
		b.	Multi-function workers
6.	Finance/Accounting	a.	Flexible budgeting
		b.	Timely and accurate cost information
7.	Purchasing	a.	Reliable vendor network with minimum lead times and perfect quality
		b.	Vendor value engineering
		c.	JIT deliveries
8.	Management Information Systems	a.	Timely and accurate systems
		b.	User-friendly systems
		c.	Change sensitive and immediately reactive systems
9.	Production- Inventory Control	a.	Short production lead times
		b.	Small lot sizes
		c.	Minimum inventory levels
10.	Top Management	a.	Commitment
		b.	Leadership
		c.	Strategic Planning

Example

One company found that its accounting systems had to be completely changed as a result of implementing JIT/ZI. The old system did not allow for new accounts payable procedures based on shipping notices and blanket purchase orders. Nor did the costing system reflect overhead absorbed in inventory as an expense. The old system encouraged building, not reducing, inventories because accumulated inventory was an asset. The new system treats all overhead as an expense and values inventory based only on its' variable material and labor costs.

The pursuit of eliminating inventories requires system-wide integration that is more advanced than that required for MRP systems as discussed in Chapter 4. As a result, presenting or implementing JIT/ZI in a logical order is difficult because every aspect of the production/inventory system interacts with every other aspect of the organization.

JIT/ZI Philosophy and Goals

To appreciate the JIT/ZI philosophy, it is helpful to review the culture in which this approach was developed. The JIT/ZI crusade was imported from Japan in the early 1980's. Space and resources command a premium in Japan. It is an overpopulated nation with few natural resources where most raw materials and energy-producing goods are imported. Since Japan's economy was severely damaged in World War II, it needed hard currency to rebuild and chose to acquire this currency by exporting high-volume consumer products to foreign markets. Japan's transportation and raw material cost disadvantages, coupled with its relatively scarce space, forced a focus on waste elimination as a key to national, industry, company, and individual prosperities.

Out of this cultural context the never-be-satisfied philosophy of waste elimination was born. The philosophy of JIT/ZI is simple: the elimination of all wastes. This philosophy views inventories as evil and wasteful. Inventories not only are resources not being used but are slack or fat that cover up other wasteful areas in a company. The optimum level of inventory is not the level that covers the bumps or problem areas with some statistical level of confidence but, rather, the optimum level is zero inventory. Inventories can only be eliminated if the reasons for inventories (as discussed in Chapter 2) are removed. Reaching the zero inventory level would be possible only under the following conditions:

1. Low or insignificant set-up (or order) times and costs.
2. Lot sizes equal to one.
3. Minimum and almost instantaneous lead times.
4. Balanced and level work loads.
5. No interruptions due to poor quality, unscheduled equipment downtimes, engineering changes, or other unplanned changes.

As discussed in Chapter 2, inventories are carried in virtually all systems precisely because these idealized conditions do not exist. The JIT/ZI approach connotes a level of perfection that is unattainable. However, it stimulates a quest for constant improvement in the environmental conditions that necessitate inventories.

JIT/ZI is a journey, not a destination, toward continuous improvement. This elimination of inventories is achieved with the following process:

1. Inventories are reduced until a problem (bump) is discovered and identified.
2. Once the problem is defined, the inventory level is increased to absorb the shock of this bump and to keep the system operating smoothly.
3. The problem is analyzed and practical ways are identified to reduce or remove the problem.
4. Once the problem is reduced or removed, the inventory level is reduced until another problem is discovered and identified.
5. Steps 2 through 4 of the process are repeated until the minimum possible level of inventories is achieved.

In this iterative way, getting rid of inventory uncovers problems and stimulates the search for practical ways to get rid of the problems so that continuous improvement in ridding the system of wastes can be made. In the next section, the organizational and operational prerequisites to implementing a JIT/ZI approach are discussed.

Organizational and Operational Prerequisites to Implementing JIT/ZI

Organizational Prerequisites

There are three organizational prerequisite conditions that must be present for a JIT/ZI management approach to succeed:

1. An organizational strategy focused on low-cost, high-quality production.
2. An organizational culture that promotes trust, teamwork and the habit of improvement.
3. A supportive top management.

The impetus for JIT/ZI is the increased competitive nature of our marketplace. Low-cost, high-quality competitive strategies by Japanese and U.S. firms have been successful in capturing markets in the electronics, automotive, steel, and other high-volume, repetitive industries. While JIT/ZI applies, in concept, to any kind of organization, it has its greatest impact and potential contribution in repetitive manufacturing environments. The strategic goal must be to capture the effects of an automated repetitive system. Thus, parts of JIT/ZI may be applied to, and provide some benefits for, a customized job shop manufacturer, but it is not likely to be strategically important. Similarly, the JIT/ZI concepts have not found fertile ground in companies emphasizing customized service and flexibility to meet a variety of needs. There is some evidence that the JIT/ZI concepts related to raw materials are beginning to be adopted by high-volume, standardized services to control material costs.

Recent research has shown that successful companies have dominant and coherent cultures.[2] Successful implementation of the JIT/ZI approach requires a corporate culture characterized by the following factors:

1. Habit of improvement and never-be-satisfied attitude. As Zero Inventory is an unattainable goal or end, management and workers must share an attitude that the Japanese call "pursuing the last grain of rice." This attitude promotes and reflects a quest of excellence and of not being satisfied with less than the ideal of Zero Inventories.
2. Long term instead of short term. The quest for continuous improvements, however small, can only be justified in the

long term. The JIT/ZI approach sacrifices the short-term costs of removing or solving problems for the long-term savings from not needing inventory.

3. Total quality/productivity concept. Poor quality represents waste, interrupts production, and requires inventory. Zero defect programs, from raw materials through finished goods, get rid of this waste and increase productivity.

4. Systems that are people systems. Highly integrated systems such as JIT/ZI require skilled teamwork, trust, cooperation, and personnel development. The pursuit of the ideal level of zero inventories can not be accomplished unless workers and managers work together for continuous improvement.

5. Manufacturing discipline. Zero inventories require minimum disruptions. Manufacturing planning and execution demands discipline to minimize these disruptions. Further, everyone must pay attention to details, have the discipline to perform their jobs as expected, and have the autonomy to identify deviations from plans.

6. Interdepartmental coordination. The organizational structure, rules, procedures, and policies should promote interdepartmental coordination. Reducing inventories will likely cut across several departments.

Top management must understand what JIT/ZI is, how it supports the strategy of the company, and their role in providing support for implementation. The top management role is primarily one of managing the culture of the company. Top management must communicate a vision of the why, who, what, when, and how of JIT/ZI. Top management must provide moral and organizational support in the form of education, training, and staff support for JIT/ZI related changes. Top management must design appropriate organizational structures and adopt the appropriate leadership style.

Example

The corporate director of materials and purchasing of a large electronics firm characterized their JIT/ZI program as a cultural program—not an inventory program. According to him, "Our program has attempted to change the way people view problems so that

problems become opportunities for improvement. This program
represents our new strategic approach, and helping everyone
understand what it is and why it is important has been foremost in
the minds of top management."
    Because the JIT/ZI program was strategically important for the
company and because it cut across departments, a division general manager was appointed as the leader or "champion" of its
implementation in that division.

Regrettably, too few organizations recognize or understand that
these organizational prerequisites must be in place before JIT/ZI
operational changes can be attempted. Most top managers view JIT/ZI
as another set of techniques, and they expect materials managers to
implement these concepts without making the necessary organizational
changes. Where these organizational prerequisites are not present
and where there is little likelihood of them being changed, JIT/ZI
will not be successful.

Operational Prerequisites

There are six operational prerequisites for JIT/ZI including:

1. Flow (repetitive) design.
2. Process flexibility.
3. Quality processes and output.
4. Multi-function operations.
5. Smooth and balanced production.
6. Reliable vendor networks.

It should be noted that while changes in these conditions are beyond
the control of the inventory manager, they do represent the problem
areas (or bumps) in the system for which inventories may be carried.

Flow (Repetitive) Design: Designing the product and the process for
flow (repetitive) production is the first operational prerequisite of
JIT/ZI. Many organizations operate an intermittent, customized job
shop even when some or even much of the work flows through the
system in a similar way. Designing for flow production involves product design and process design.
    Product design is the starting point for accomplishing repetitive

production, inasmuch as products may be designed for produceability. The number of materials or parts should be minimized and the combinations in which these parts are manufactured should be limited. As the number of parts increases, so do the required inventories and the production processes. Product variety may be accomplished by using modules that may be put together in different combinations to meet market-driven variety needs. The Palm Beach mix and match sport coats and slacks line is an example of this modularization. Value analysis and computer-aided design (CAD) techniques can be used as practical ways to enhance the produceability of products and, thereby, reduce inventory needs.

The process and layout of the process is a function of the product design. If the product mix consists of highly standardized products, the process and layout is straightforward. For the JIT/ZI approach, the process layout should approach the effects of an assembly line even if one does not exist. This will provide for a smooth flow of materials through the system without building inventories in queues and can be achieved in two ways. First, the operations may be divided, or focused, and dedicated as lines that produce families of similar products. Second, all machines or processes required across similar products can be grouped into work cells. This technique of group technology is not new and has been referred to as the "poor man's assembly line." Group technology may reduce lead times and work-in-process inventories when similar process requirements of products and/or parts exist.

Process Flexibility: Process flexibility is a crucially important operational prerequisite, if inventories are to be minimized under conditions of varied product mixes. Multiple products/parts production requires process flexibility to minimize inventories. Process flexibility is achieved by reducing setup times and having flexible automation.

Without the process flexibility of short setup times, one could not simultaneously maintain low inventories and meet customer demand while at the same time sufficiently utilizing capacity. A realistic objective of a setup reduction program is an 80% reduction in setup times in the first year. Setup time reduction programs are similar to other industrial engineering methods improvement programs. The ultimate objective in JIT/ZI is to automate setups as well as processes.

Flexible automation of material handling, setups, and operations allows for minimum inventory and maximum process flexibility to produce a wide range of similar parts and products. It is estimated that up to 80% of U.S. manufacturing is characterized by small lot batches of less than 100 units. These systems do not produce a sufficiently high volume to economically justify setting up process flow lines for each production run. However, these systems may achieve the effects of repetitive manufacturing with flexible manufacturing systems (FMS). FMS is defined as groups of computerized numerical control (CNC) equipment linked by automated material handling systems and integrated through a centralized computer to randomly manufacture a wide range of similar parts. The flexibility of these automated systems comes from the use of computers to control reprogrammable robots and CNC equipment. Variations in mix of orders, parts, routings, designs, and volume can be accommodated through the computer control system.

Quality Processes and Output: High-quality output has become strategically important not only from a marketing viewpoint but also from a production and inventory management perspective. Poor-quality output is expensive because, not only are there the direct costs of the labor, materials, and overhead of producing a defective part, but there are productivity costs. Productivity is reduced because defects require higher inventories, interrupt production, and require more overhead to control the inventories, production changes, and quality control activities caused by poor quality.

Most companies have discarded the myth that there is a tradeoff between quality and quantity. The total quality control concept has been widely adopted, and it has resulted in reducing inventories by building quality into the product as opposed to "inspecting quality in." This concept makes quality everyone's responsibility from product design through plant floor operation. The total quality control concept requires zero defects in raw material inputs and in operational processes so that zero defect outputs are produced. Zero Inventories, Just-In-Time and Zero Defects go hand in hand as total system programs.

Statistical quality control methods are used in a total quality control system to monitor all aspects of the production system. If all parts of the system are in control, then inventories are not needed to absorb quality problems. Simple process control charts are used to monitor process performance and to identify the sources of variances or deviations of output, which may be caused by tool wear, machine operations, set-up maladjustments, materials inconsistency, operator problems, or unknown (random) reasons. The idea is to use the statistical process control charts to reduce these variances until only the unknown or random sources remain. Then, if the output is not within tolerance limits, the probability of something being wrong and needing correction is 100%. This leads to the idea of controlling quality at the source. In Toyota, this idea has been implemented with what is called Jidoka, or "stop everything when something goes wrong." Instead of using inspectors, each operator is responsible for quality work. If anything goes wrong, the operator can push a button and stop a production line until the problem causing the defect is corrected.[3]

The total quality concept emphasizes preventive maintenance instead of repair maintenance. The reason for this emphasis is that repair maintenance occurs after a problem arises. Thus, inventories are needed to absorb the resulting defects and equipment downtime. With preventive maintenance, poor quality is never produced due to equipment problems and equipment never has unscheduled downtime.

Multi-function Operators: As indicated above, operators in a JIT/ZI system must be multifunctional, disciplined, and constantly looking for ways to improve the system. The presence of the organizational prerequisites determines whether the necessary environmental conditions exist to foster this kind of human resource. Even if the organizational prerequisites are present, there must be operational prerequisites related to job design, job methods and work improvement programs.

The JIT/ZI approach requires a work force that is responsible not only for the process operations but also for setups, quality inspection and control, preventive maintenance, and productivity improvement analysis and recommendations. This means the operators must be cross-trained and willing to perform multifunctional jobs that are relatively unrestricted in job classification. In order for operators to perform these multifunctional jobs efficiently and with little or no variation in time standards, standardized job methods must be followed rigidly. Standardized methods result in more predictable levels of output. If the output rate among operations is highly predictable, the work load among operations may be more easily balanced. The result of this standardization is the elimination of inventories used to decouple operations. If the standardized methods can be improved, operators are encouraged informally and formally to participate in work (productivity) improvement programs. Quality circles, operator suggestion systems, and traditional industrial engineering studies are used to make operations more productive, which in turn reduces inventory.

Smooth and Balanced Production: The JIT/ZI approach requires that production flow as smoothly as possible in the shop. This is facilitated and greatly determined by the presence of the previously discussed operational prerequisites. Smooth and balanced production requires the following conditions:

1. Uniform plant loading.
2. Minimum lot sizes.
3. Minimum lead times.
4. Pull systems.

Uniform plant loading is the starting point for zero inventories in a smooth and balanced production system. The ideal is to execute a level schedule so that there is an even distribution of material and labor requirements. To accomplish this, smooth or level production schedules of finished goods must be planned and frozen for some period in the future. Then, each day in this period, the same mix of products can be produced to meet market demand rates. This uniform output rate is used to determine the capacity needed at work centers to balance the output rates within the system. In this way, materials flow smoothly through the system, and the need for finished goods, work-in-process, and raw material inventories is reduced.

Beyond the frozen schedule, there is the suggested schedule. Thus, a two-month suggested schedule would be used to develop the monthly frozen schedule as each month rolled forward. This rolling schedule allows uniform plant loads to be replanned in response to market demand and already frozen production plans.

Uniform plant loading, capacity balance, and flexibility to meet changing market demand depend on minimum setup times. Reduced setup times also reduce lot sizes. If setup times and costs are reduced, then the lot size economics discussed in Chapter 2 would dictate smaller lot sizes. The objective of JIT/ZI is for lot sizes to approach one. Small lot sizes provide increased ability to match market demand with planned production. Small lot sizes also make quality control easier since inspections can be reduced to just two items — the first and the last.

Smoothing production and simultaneously matching production to market demands, without building inventories, requires minimizing lead time. Lead time consists of the following components: order preparation, purchasing, receiving, tooling, moving, queuing, processing, and distribution. The processing time component is usually a very small percentage of the total time. Lead times may be shortened by instituting programs to reduce the time associated with each of the components. Long lead times result in higher WIP inventories and higher WIP inventories cause long queues. Thus, controlling the amount of work released through uniform and balanced plant loading will reduce WIP and in turn reduce lead times. Reduced lead times increase forecast accuracy and enhance response to changing market demands. Reducing forecast inaccuracy translates into reducing pipeline and buffer inventories. Faster response to market changes allows for reductions in finished goods and other pipeline inventories.

The execution of smoothly flowing production is accomplished with a pull system, where material is produced in response to downstream operation needs. Material is not produced based on a planned schedule and pushed downstream but is, instead, produced based on the pull of downstream operations. The final assembly schedule pulls the subassemblies, which pull the component parts, and so forth. The pull system can be viewed as a vacuum pipeline. As material is withdrawn at one end of the pipeline, material is drawn through the pipeline. Material movement is synchronized to the rate at which it is withdrawn at the end of the pipeline.

The objective of the pipeline pull system is to reduce the pipeline stock and to increase the frequency at which material is withdrawn. As the pipeline inventory is reduced and the withdrawal frequency is increased, the pull system becomes an integrated inventory and production scheduling system.

In the Toyota system, this pull effect is accomplished with the use of Kanban cards.[3] Move Kanbans authorize the movement of material between work centers. These cards circulate between the outbound stockpoint of the supplier work center and the inbound stockpoint of the user work center. Each card is attached to a standard container. Production Kanbans authorize the production of standard containers to replace containers removed from the outbound stockpoints by Move Kanbans. Production Kanbans are used at the work centers and include information such as the part number to be produced, a short bill of materials, and stockpoints from where bill of materials parts are obtained. Unattached Production Kanbans authorize production and unattached Move Kanbans authorize withdrawing parts. Parts are never produced nor moved in quantities in excess of that needed and provided by the standard container size. The size of the pipeline inventory is a function of the number of cards (or containers) and the frequency at which containers are moved.

The JIT/ZI approach is to remove a Move Kanban (thereby reducing inventory) and observe if a problem occurs. If one occurs, it is identified and the Move Kanban is replaced until the problem is solved. Once the problem is solved, the Move Kanban is removed, and the process is repeated until inventory reductions are no longer possible. In addition, the size of the container is a function of the economic lot size. As set-up times (costs) are reduced, the economic lot size and container size are reduced.

Reliable Vendor Networks: The JIT/ZI purchasing idea is one-at-a-time continuous delivery. Vendors are needed who can make frequent deliveries of small lot sizes in standard containers with zero defects. Raw material inventories may be eliminated if delivery lead times approach zero and the exact quantity with zero defects is delivered. To accomplish this, vendors must:

1. Be geographically close.
2. Know the material requirements over time.
3. Cooperate with the buyer in product design, purchase management, and quality control.

In Japan, most vendors make a small variety of parts for a single customer and are located geographically close to the customer. The material requirements of the customer are delivered exactly when needed; even up to the minute in some cases. The vendor's destiny is tied to the customer's destiny so a close relationship exists in improving product costs and in providing zero defects. Purchasing, receiving, and inspection are relatively paperless and built on trust and mutual interests.

JIT/ZI purchasing is one of the most difficult operational prerequisites for U.S. manufacturers. Vendor-customer relationships historically have been largely adversarial. However, JIT/ZI purchasing successes have been reported by Kawasaki-USA, Hewlett-Packard, IBM, and other firms. Single source vendors, weekly truck deliveries instead of railcar deliveries, and consolidation warehouses are examples of U.S. responses to JIT/ZI purchasing.

JIT/ZI Implementations and Results

There is no way of knowing how many companies are engaged in implementing JIT/ZI. As was the case in the 1970's with MRP, virtually every medium- to large-size and most small manufacturers are contemplating this new approach. Undoubtedly, the results achieved by those implementing this approach are a function of how efficiently this organizational change is managed. Exhibits 7-1 to 7-4 provide a sample of results, reported in another study, of companies in various states of JIT/ZI implementation.[3]

Exhibit 7-1
Results of JIT/ZI Programs in Japan

Company	Duration of Program	Inventory Reduction	Labor Productivity Increase
A	3 years	45%	50%
B	3 years	16%	80%
C	4 years	30%	60%
D	2 years	20%	50%

Exhibit 7-2
Japanese Versus U.S. Inventory Turnover Ratios: Selected Industries

Industry	Japan 1970	Japan 1978	Japan % Change	U.S 1970	U.S 1978	U.S % Change
Auto and truck	9.2	11.9	29%	4.3	5.6	30%
Auto parts	6.3	11.3	79%	3.2	3.9	22%
Electronics	4.6	6.0	30%	3.6	3.2	(11%)
Construction equipment	2.8	3.0	7%	3.7	3.2	(14%)

Exhibit 7-3
Jidosha Kiki Company, Ltd.

JIT/ZI Measures	Start of Program 1976	1981	Percent Improvement
Inventory (days on hand)			
Raw materials	3.1	1.0	68%
Purchased parts	3.8	1.2	68
Work-in-process	4.0	1.0	75
Finished goods	8.6	3.7	57
Defects			
From suppliers	2.6%	.11%	96%
Internally	.34%	.01%	97
Setup times			
Over 60 minutes	20%	0%	100%
100 seconds to 60 minutes	80%	38%	53
Under 100 seconds	0%	62%	–

Exhibit 7-4
U.S. Plants: JIT/ZI Results, 1982

Company	Inventory Reduction
General Motors-Pontiac	70% work-in-process reduction of intake manifolds in nine months
General Motors-Oldsmobile	65% reduction in bumper parts inventory
Westinghouse (Bloomington)	60% ($30,000) inventory reduction of throw-out switch parts
Hewlett-Packard (Vancouver)	30% reduction in parts

These results indicate that not only Japanese but U.S. firms can benefit from the JIT/ZI approach. The following examples illustrate how JIT/ZI was implemented and the results that were achieved in, first, a large Japanese plant and, second, a small U.S. plant.

Case 1: Toyo Kogyo Co. Ltd.'s "New Production System" [4]

The year 1986 was the year of the "New Production System" (NPS) for Toyo Kogyo Co. Ltd. (makers of Mazda cars and trucks). The decade of the 1970s had begun with promise of rapid growth and financial prosperity. Toyo Kogyo (TK) had carved out a market niche in the worldwide automobile market with a mass-produced rotary engine automobile. In 1971, the Mazda was the "Car of the Year" and, by 1973, sales in the United States had grown to about 120,000 cars. Eighty percent of the TK cars sold in the United States had rotary engines.

A highly integrated and modern auto plant had been developed to produce TK cars. The production operation included four divisions: founding and forging, engine, body, and painting and assembly. On-line, real-time computerized scheduling of mixed model assemblies, high-technology processes, and material handling had been financed largely through debt equity.

In 1973, the oil shock precipitated the slide for TK. Mazda cars were not energy efficient nor were they efficiently produced. From 1973 to 1975, Mazda U.S. sales plummeted 70% and TK suffered an operating loss of about $58 million. The pressure to survive fell heavily on cutting manufacturing costs and reducing lead times. One of the principle objectives of the NPS was to lower work-in-process inventory by 50%. By 1976, work-in-process had been reduced by 10%; however, there was resistance to further reductions because utilization efficiencies were falling and schedules were being disrupted. Mr. Yamasaki, executive director, recognized that to reduce inventories further required radical changes. Programs were instituted to: reduce set-up times, improve material handling, improve preventive maintenance, reduce lot sizes, improve the layout, eliminate defects, use Kanbans to pull work through the system, train workers to be multifunctional, and level the monthly production schedules. In addition to these operational changes, Mr. Yamasaki provided top management support and commitment to the philosophy of turning problems into opportunities to eliminate waste.

By 1979, work-in-process inventory had been reduced from five days to about 2.7 days of production, while annual production had increased from over 716,000 to more than one million. That Toyo Kogyo was able to survive financially is due, in large part, to the success of the JIT/ZI approach of the new production system.

Case 2: General Electric Asheboro Housewares Plant[5]

The General Electric Asheboro Plant is relatively small, with less than 500 nonunion employees producing small consumer products. About 20,000 units of various models of coffeemakers, toaster ovens, irons, hair dryers, and heating pads are produced daily.

As early as 1980, Asheboro's management was learning about JIT/ZI through an information exchange between GE and Toyota Motor Company. In 1982, the plant needed more space for additional product lines, and plant management decided that the JIT/ZI approach could free up the space needed. At GE, JIT/ZI is seen as a broad manufacturing philosophy focusing on eliminating waste and freeing up resources. It is recognized that JIT/ZI requires significant plant organizational and operational changes. As a result, the move toward JIT/ZI at a plant is voluntary. By 1984, over 40 GE plants had adopted JIT/ZI programs.

The JIT/ZI work was focused on the highest volume product, the coffeemaker. A super line was created for mixed-model assembly of coffeemakers. This redesigned line required more stations than older lines and uncovered the first inventory problem. Historically, a week's worth of parts was stocked at the assembly line. This new line with more work stations would have dramatically increased the work-in-process except that only one day's worth of parts was allowed to stock the line which, in turn, required changes in the way work was scheduled and transported from contributing areas. In addition, spaces and bins were designated for everything needed, and the appearance of each work station was upgraded.

Educational programs were instituted for management and workers, and already existing quality circles were used to communicate JIT/ZI ideas. As more JIT/ZI ideas were introduced, quality became the focus of attention. Operators were trained to be responsible for 100% inspection and for posting statistical quality control charts. In addition, error-proofing devices, such as different colored lights, were installed to signal when help at a work station was needed.

The success achieved on the coffeemaker line encouraged expansion of the JIT/ZI concept throughout the plant. Programs were instituted to reduce set-up times and lot sizes, to relocate contributing areas adjacent to assembly lines, and to deliver materials daily directly to the assembly lines. While achieving the original goal of freeing floor space of over 50,000 square feet, additional JIT contributions in the first year included other items as listed below.

Performance Measure	Percent Improvement
Direct labor productivity	15
Indirect labor productivity	25
Inventory	40
Scrap and rework	33

Survey Results

For the 21 survey respondents with JIT/ZI systems, a variety of programs were identified. These programs are called different names, including total quality control, total quality improvement, and productivity improvement, as well as the traditional names of Just-In-Time and/or Zero Inventories. At the time of the survey, these programs had been implemented from less than six months up to three years, with an average duration of 18 to 24 months. These programs were being implemented in low volume, job shop layouts (32%), high volume, repetitive layouts (37%), and layouts combining both low and high volumes.

Follow-up telephone interviews confirmed that the respondents have widely varying definitions of JIT/ZI, and they have selectively implemented pieces of the total JIT/ZI system to meet their most pressing problems. One firm defined JIT as a raw materials purchasing system and concentrated strictly on reducing vendor lead times and increasing vendor quality. Another firm defined JIT as a finished goods inventory reduction system and focused its effort on reducing finished goods safety stock. The majority of the responding firms seem to be focusing on the work-in-process-related operational characteristics.

Responding firms reported the most progress in reducing lot sizes, increasing control through visibility, using blanket purchase orders, reducing vendor lead times, and developing and educating managers and operators. They reported relatively little progress in improving sales forecasts, product design, automation, preventive maintenance, or pulling work through the system.

The greatest benefits reported are consistent with the progress areas cited above. Not surprisingly, the greatest improvements and benefits are related to reducing WIP inventory and safety stock of raw materials. These reductions translate into increased inventory turnover ratios, particularly for WIP. The least improvement, or smallest benefits, reported included reductions in finished goods and safety stock inventories, improvements in interdepartmental coordination and morale, and improvements in production scheduling and plant efficiency. The degrees of improvement achieved in selected performance measures are shown in Exhibit 7-5.

Exhibit 7-5
Percent of Degree of Improvement in Performance Measures
for 21 JIT Systems Surveyed

	Degree of Improvement				
Performance Measure	Little/ None = 1	Some = 2	Much = 3	Very Much = 4	Average Improvement
a. Reduced inventory					
(1.) Materials	11%	11%	33%	44%	2.1
(2.) Work-in-process	-	17	28	56	2.4
(3.) Finished goods	17	44	17	22	1.4
b. Reduced safety stock					
(1.) Materials	-	11	50	39	2.3
(2.) Work-in-process	-	6	47	47	2.4
(3.) Finished goods	18	24	29	29	1.7
c. Better production scheduling	17	17	50	17	1.7
d. Improved plant efficiency	17	28	28	28	1.7
e. Improved morale	17	33	39	11	1.4
f. Improved coordination among sales, production and engineering	11	56	17	17	1.4

The most important factor in achieving these results has to do with top management leadership and support. Several respondents stressed the need for a "champion" from top management in order to change the traditional culture. This champion came from accounting in one firm, from finance in another, and from manufacturing in several firms. Not surprisingly, the most frequently cited problem for successful implementations was getting people to believe in and to adopt the JIT philosophy.

Surprisingly, the cost of the JIT changes was not reported as a significant problem, even for one firm where the costs to date are in excess of several million dollars. Forty-six percent of the respondents reported costs to date of less than $50,000. This relatively low cost figure is consistent with the previously cited lack of progress in automation. Apparently, firms are implementing JIT principles, with their existing plant and equipment, before moving toward automated systems.

Several firms that had not adopted the JIT/ZI approach for their companies cited the lack of cost/benefit, or the excess costs involved in such a move, as reasons. Obviously, the firms that had adopted such an approach found the costs not to be excessive and a very favorable cost/benefit existed. Lack of top management support or interest was another common reason for lack of implementation.

Not one firm implementing JIT/ZI indicated that a return-on-investment (ROI) analysis had been performed. In follow-up telephone interviews, several indicated that top management may have done ROI analysis, but the JIT/ZI implementation was a strategic move and, as such, it was difficult to measure in terms of cost flows. Virtually every respondent interviewed indicated that their accounting and financial systems were at best meaningless and at worst counter-productive to JIT/ZI implementation.

Summary

Just-In-Time/Zero Inventory is a relatively new approach to managing inventories. While its focus is on reducing inventories to zero levels, the underlying philosophy is to get rid of all wastes in the system. As such, it is more than an inventory management approach; it is a total system management approach. Inventory reduction is the means of uncovering wasteful characteristics of the system. These problems are viewed as opportunities for improvements. While zero inventories is an unattainable goal, it is the means of continuous improvement and achievement of manufacturing excellence.

JIT/ZI programs require organization and operational changes to be successfully implemented. The culture of the organization must be changed to one of viewing problems as opportunities for improvement. Top management leadership and support are absolute prerequisites for success. All departments and functions within the organization will be affected. Considerable education and training must occur before operations are changed. Once the organizational prerequisites are in place, programs for improving operations, such as reducing set-up times and lot sizes, may be undertaken.

The results of a survey of JIT/ZI users indicate these are relatively new programs in most firms and are viewed as total system programs that are strategically important to the firm. Because of this, top management leadership and support, primarily in the form of education and training, are viewed as the most critical factors of success.

Dramatic improvements in performance, particularly in WIP and raw materials inventory levels, are reported. These systems are being implemented without supporting financial and accounting systems. The impact of JIT/ZI and increased automation implementation on accounting systems is discussed in the next chapter.

Notes

[1] Buffa, Edward, *Meeting the Competitive Challenge*, New York: Dow Jones-Irvin, 1984.

[2] Peters, Thomas J. and Robert H. Waterman, Jr., *In Search of Excellence*, New York: Harper & Row, 1982.

[3] Hall, Robert W., *Zero Inventories*, New York: Dow Jones-Irvin, 1983.

[4] Abstracted from *Toyo Kogyo Co. Ltd (A) and (B)*, Harvard Business School Case Nos. 9-682-092 and 0-682-093, copyright ©1982.

[5] Abstracted from Spurgeon, Edward V., "Just-In-Time Implementation: Job Shop Versus Flow Shop," *Readings in Zero Inventory*, APICS 27th Annual International Conference, October 9-12, 1984, pp. 88-89.

Chapter 8

Implications of Future Inventory Systems for Accounting

What happens to an accounting function when a company adopts a JIT/ZI production philosophy and purposely attempts to reduce inventory to a zero level? Since the entire production process undergoes a change, what impact does a zero inventory system have on the accounting concept of a product cost (which usually involves the allocation of overhead or burden)? Are the definitions of cost themselves changed? Is direct labor a meaningful idea for the calculation of product costs or are all costs, other than materials, a period cost or expense? How is product cost calculated when materials are the only significant variable cost? Are the current arguments for including fixed cost as part of the product cost valid when almost all costs are fixed costs?

From the results of the study, it would seem that many accountants are not aware of the potential impacts of implementing Just-In-Time and/or automated systems. The potential impact on the accounting function of the JIT/ZI systems and of computerized automation in the factory has not been thoroughly considered by many accounting managers. This is also an area that is almost ignored in the current literature. Because accountants may not be heavily involved in such systems, manufacturing personnel are not overly concerned with the accounting function and the changes needed for accounting to provide adequate data and information to the other functions of a company.

Perhaps because of the lack of involvement in the design and implementation of such systems, the accounting profession seems to have paid little attention to the problems such systems can present to the accounting function. The observations presented in this chapter are tentative since there are little or no empirical data on which to base conclusions. The observations presented are based on the comments provided by the participants in this study, on recent experiences of the authors, and the writings of a few authors.[1]

143

Areas Affected by the JIT/ZI Systems

There would seem to be at least four major accounting areas affected when JIT/ZI or computerized automated systems are installed in a factory: the changing nature of direct costs; the increase in overhead costs; the shift in the number and nature of transactions that have to be processed by the accounting function; and the rearrangement of the flow of materials, parts, or products, which may require redefinition of the responsibility-center concept. Each of these is explored in more depth.

Changing Nature of Direct Costs

When the JIT/ZI, or computerized automated systems, are installed in a manufacturing company, direct labor costs are reduced. As the degree of automation is increased, direct labor costs are reduced and the amount of overhead increased. As operators take on additional nondirect tasks of setting up, preventive maintenance and inspecting and, as excess capacity is traded off against inventory by smoothing production and by maintaining a relatively constant labor force, labor costs are accumulated in total and become fixed instead of being accumulated by operation or work center as variable costs. In effect, labor costs and overhead both become fixed period costs. With new manufacturing technologies, variable costs may disappear, except for purchases of materials and the energy required to operate the equipment.

Example

In one of the companies included in the survey the cost account-ing manager was one of the "champions" of the JIT/ZI system installed in the company. Before installing the JIT/ZI system the company employed full absorption costing, both within the company and for external financial statements. Now the company uses direct costing throughout for internal use and full absorption for external use. Adjustments are made as needed to spread the fixed costs to the products for inventory valuation purposes. The JIT/ZI approach was the catalyst that provoked the change in the accounting system.

Increase in Overhead Costs

Unit output drives direct labor and material inputs on the shop floor that we all think of when we envision a factory. But in the factories of the future the real driving force comes from transactions, not physical products. These transactions involve exchanges of the materials and/or information necessary to move production along but do not directly result in physical products. Four basic transactions are carried out by the people whose wages and salaries are incurred because of the following types of transactions:

1. Logistical transactions — order, execute and confirm the movement of materials from one location to another.
2. Balancing transaction — ensure that the supplies of materials, labor, and capacity are equal to the demand.
3. Quality transactions — includes quality control, indirect engineering and procurement as well as the identification and communication of specifications, certification that other transactions have taken place as they were supposed to, and the development and recording of relevant data.
4. Change transactions — update basic manufacturing information systems to accommodate change in engineering designs, schedules, routing standards, materials specifications and bills of material.

These transactions account for much of the overhead costs in automated factories and often cause overhead costs to far exceed direct labor costs. Overhead costs, as a percentage of value added and as a percentage of overall manufacturing costs, have been rising steadily for more than 100 years. This may be due in part to the increasing number of transactions required to maintain the traditional cost accounting system.[2]

Change in Number and Type of Transactions Recorded by the Accounting Function

The factory has experienced great changes over the past decade and these changes are expected to continue into the future. Change, by itself, increases the number and type of transactions recorded by the accounting function, but it is not the only factor. Unlevel loads and work flows also increase the number of transactions. Every time an engineering change order is issued, a schedule breaks down, a quality problem erupts, a material has to be expedited, and so on, a wave of transactions flows through a plant. Instability in plant schedules and performances cause many plant managers to overstaff their work forces so that the plants can react to unexpected peak loads in transaction volume. The shift to a JIT/ZI philosophy will cause greater stability in the plant with a resulting decrease in the number and types of transactions. Thus, the burden rate based on transactions may have to change dramatically as a firm implements a JIT/ZI approach. This may cause some major problems for the cost accounting function since overhead is accounted for in the traditional cost system using direct labor, not transactions, as the causal factor.

Management of Flow of Products

In a plant using cost centers, data collection occupies considerable time and resources. Every time material moves from one operation to the next, data are collected that reflect how long the operation required, who performed it, and how many parts were involved. This information is used to drive payroll, cost accounting, and inventory systems. The adoption of JIT/ZI requires that the cost-center concept be replaced with a work-cell concept, with the work cells functioning very similarly to those of a small assembly line. Work cells are dedicated to the production of a limited number of parts or products requiring similar sequences of operations. While cell managers are responsible for throughput in their cells, the work must be pulled through the center from downstream user work cells. Without orders to produce, the work cell stands idle. This can result in substantial idle time for some cells in a particular plant. Under JIT/ZI operations, when a processing operation completes a batch and has no further work authorizations, it is supposed to stop until such an authorization is received. Management of the flow of products is through the management of standardized containers holding predetermined lot sizes and the management of the movement of these containers through work cells.

Potential Changes to a Traditional Cost Accounting System

Accountants are going to have to change many of the traditional cost accounting concepts if the system is to be useful in a JIT/ZI environment. Some of the more obvious changes are discussed in the paragraphs that follow.

Allocation of Overhead

Under Generally Accepted Accounting Principles or GAAP, it is necessary to allocate overhead to products. Companies may use direct labor dollars, direct labor hours, machine hours, etcetera in this allocation process. What happens when direct labor no longer meets the materiality principle? Unless there is a substantial change in the allocation process, the burden rate may increase and provide management with some misleading information. What happens to the use of accounting information when the burden rate increases from 50% to 1800%? Does the system start to lose credibility? The obvious answer is to move to a direct costing system as was done by some companies in the survey. Where full absorption costing has been used in the past, there are implications for pricing decisions, performance evaluations, and other factors. Management must reorient itself to the changing nature of the costs and the cost behaviors.

There is also the problem of product costs for external financial reporting. Under the JIT/ZI philosophy, one method of determining unit costs is to take the production costs for a period and divide them by the production for the same period of time. How would this procedure conform with Generally Accepted Accounting Principles? What changes to the procedures are necessary in order to conform to GAAP? These questions have not been fully answered.

Variance Analysis

Variances are used in many companies to measure variations or deviations from plan. These variances are calculated by comparing some standard amount with the actual amount and then deriving a rate, spending, and price variance or a usage, efficiency, and volume variance. There are many variations of such calculations in practice. The main purpose is the same: to evaluate the efficiency and effectiveness of people. Most of these use a standard quantity in the calculations, which is usually revised on a yearly basis.

In a JIT/ZI environment one must question the applicability of the traditional method of calculating variances. Remember that direct labor and overhead are fixed period costs under such a system and that direct labor includes multi-functional nondirect labor activity. Also, the quantity variance for materials may become nonmaterial since the control over the purchase of the right materials at the right time may have all but eliminated quantity variances. At least the feedback required in a JIT/ZI system has located and evaluated the quantity variance for materials long before they can be calculated and reported in a traditional accounting system. The efficiency variance for labor may also have no relevance because labor is assigned to the production of lot sizes as they are needed, and it is not calculated, or has no meaning, when it is accumulated or reported on a gross measure. The need is for the evaluation to be conducted on a lot by lot basis rather than on a plantwide or period basis. Overhead efficiency variances will follow the calculation of labor efficiency variances. Thus the same comments apply to overhead.

As information workers, such as design engineers, systems analysts, and maintenance technicians, replace traditional direct labor workers in factories, quantity measures, such as direct labor hours, may be at best irrelevant and will more likely be counterproductive to a company's manufacturing operations.

Definition of Capacity

For accountants, the definition of capacity may be completely changed under a JIT/ZI system. Capacity is usually determined after assuming some lot size or is based on the expected throughput for next year. What happens when the focus of attention is on trading off excess labor and plant capacity for reduced inventories rather than some estimated level used by the accountants in setting standards or product costs? For a JIT/ZI system, capacity has no real relevance as far as costing is concerned. The major concern is the availability of capacity to accomplish the output as reflected in a plan for next year, and it is revised as the forecasted sales is changed to reflect actual results. This capacity is used for planning purposes and not for control or costing purposes. The accountants use a capacity to allocate overhead costs by setting the direct labor burden rate. Such information may then be used for pricing or other decisions. This is a need of the accounting function that has questionable usefulness in a JIT/ZI inventory system.

Responsibility Accounting Centers

Under a JIT/ZI system work flows from one work cell to another. The concept of a work cell is different from that of a cost center since the work cell is similar to a miner assembly line and is not used to accumulate costs or to evaluate efficiency. In fact, the work cell stands idle if there is no immediate need for the output of the work cell. It may be that the cost/profit/investment centers — used for so long in the traditional cost accounting system to evaluate, to plan, and to control operations—may have no applicability in a JIT/ZI system. At least, the concept of responsibility accounting is not applicable in such systems. This area needs major attention by the accounting function.

Setting Standards

In a JIT/ZI system, what standards are meaningful? As illustrated in the paragraphs above, the need for efficiency and effectiveness standards, as calculated and evaluated in a traditional accounting system, may not be applicable to a JIT/ZI system. One may then ask what standards are relevant if a JIT/ZI system is adopted. While the answers to these questions probably are not yet fully defined for most companies using a JIT/ZI system, there would seem to be some general types of standards that are applicable both to the accounting function and to the production function. Some of these standards are considered in the paragraphs that follow.

Waste and scrap standards. These types of standards allow management to highlight some of the factors that influence cost while, at the same time, permitting shop management to identify potential reasons or bumps in the JIT/ZI system. These may be stated in quantities for the production personnel and in dollars for the accounting function. This is a common component of standards in many manufacturing environments today, and there would seem to be little change in this type of standard in a JIT/ZI environment. The only major shift may be in the calculation of the variance. It is important that provisions be made to allow frequent revisions in this standard as the zero inventory system is improved over time. One of the objectives of such a system is to remove all waste and scrap from the system.

Price variances for material. While there may not be a need for the calculation of price variances for labor and overhead, there would still seem to be a need for the evaluation of the purchasing function by calculating and evaluating the rationale underlying the price variance for purchased materials.

Earned hours and actual hours. It is important in a JIT/ZI system to control both the quality and quantity of output, since quality and quantity both impact on the throughput and influence the quantity and type of materials, labor, and overhead needed in the production process. Therefore, the comparison of earned hours and actual hours may be useful information if management is to plan and control the production process. The emphasis is on the maximization of throughput rather than on the maximization of earned hours. The definition of earned hours may need to be changed to include some traditionally nondirect hours. The ratio of earned hours/actual hours needs to be evaluated in terms of the flow of material, labor, and overhead on the production line. That is to say, earned hours should not be used to build inventory if the building of inventory is not within the plan established by management.

Other Problem Areas for Accountants

Budgets

The concept of a flexible budget has been illustrated many times using the manufacturing environment as an example. This concept may not have substantial validity if the direct labor and overhead are fixed and sunk costs and materials are closely planned and controlled. In that type of environment, a fixed budget may be more appropriate for direct labor and overhead, since these factors of production are assigned based on need and lot sizes and not on volume of production produced. While a flexible budget may be used for materials, the key item is to control the price and quantity based on the need over the planning horizon. Variations based on flexible budgets may not disclose any particularly useful information to management.

Pricing

In some companies the product costs, as developed by the accounting function and based on standard costs or other estimates, are one of the major factors entering into pricing decisions. Even where market prices may be the most important factor, costs do provide a basis for evaluation of the profitability or nonprofitability of a particular product and may lead to some decisions on the desirability of capacity and market share expansion. What happens when the variable product costs are based only on materials and all direct labor and overhead are treated as fixed, sunk costs? This may lead to a complete change in the establishment of pricing policies. The selling price may not change, the profit may not change, but the evaluation of the profitability of a particular product may have to be reevaluated.

Expediting Costs

The effective installation of a JIT/ZI system requires producing to a plan and "freezing" that plan to minimize schedule changes. (This is also the philosophy underlying the MRP system discussed earlier.) The question becomes one of who is responsible for schedule changes and the interruption costs incurred for schedule changes — marketing or production? In the traditional system these costs are frequently buried in the production area and are difficult to isolate. They may show up as part of some unexplained variance.

Taxes

One of the most obvious impacts a JIT/ZI system may have is on the taxes paid when the inventory items are reduced. This is particularly true if the company has been using the LIFO method of inventory valuation. In some extreme cases the additional taxes due may offset some of the immediate cost advantages from using a system. However, even in those cases where the taxes are substantially increased, the other benefits should still suggest that the JIT/ZI philosophy may be in the best long-run interests of the company. A company should plan the installation of such a system in order to minimize the long-run impact of taxes if these are a material issue.

Example

The accountant of one company using a JIT/ZI system stated that in his firm corporate management was responsible for the management of inventories from the viewpoint of taxes. The responsibility of each plant was to produce to the plan developed by the corporate staff. Tax avoidance measures did not come under the authority of the plant manager or accountant.

Many companies using a standard cost system report inventories to corporate staff on a standard cost or FIFO basis and then the corporate staff adjusts these to a LIFO basis for financial and tax reporting. Assuming this to be a common practice, the adjustment to a JIT/ZI system would present no tax problems at the plant level, although the problems may be very material on the corporate level.

Companies adopting a JIT/ZI system, or any good inventory management system, should expect their inventories to be reduced when compared with the existing system. The Thor Power Co. Case is the leading case in deciding how and when excess inventory may be deducted for tax purposes. General rules state that companies must dispose of this excess inventory in some manner before it may be deducted for income tax purposes. Companies with excess inventory should consider the implications of this tax court case very carefully.[3]

Evaluation of Inventory Under JIT/ZI

In many of the companies sampled in this study, the increases in inventory turns were one of the most visible and dramatic examples of the effect of such systems on the level of inventory dollars. On average, inventory turns doubled for the responding firms. For those companies using inventory turnover as a guide to evaluation of the level of management efficiency and effectiveness, this shift in the level of turns required a rethinking of the standard or level of comparison. What were acceptable turnovers in the past are now unacceptable. This has some potential conflicts since acceptable performance is now undefined as far as ratios are concerned. Because different companies in the same industry may or may not use JIT/ZI techniques, or are at different stages of development of such systems, published inventory turnovers should be used with caution since they may or may not be comparable.

In responses to the two questionnaires, inventory turns were most often used by the accountants or by upper management as the standard for measuring inventory management performance. Increased ratios or turns may be used as a primary objective for a JIT/ZI implementation. An objective of doubling turns in two years may be appropriate. Whatever the exact increase, the real test is whether turns continuously improve. Inventory turns are absolute measures and if, after installing a JIT/ZI system, the turns do not dramatically increase, then additional investigation is warranted. New and higher standards will be necessary to evaluate the ongoing improvement in managing inventories. The use of turns is a very useful device in short-run evaluation. Each firm will have to set its own objectives for turns depending on its progress in installing a JIT/ZI system and on the competitiveness in their industry.

Summary

Implementing JIT/ZI inventory systems in a manufacturing environment almost certainly means major changes throughout a company. Many of those changes affect the cost accounting systems currently in place. This chapter has attempted to detail some of the more obvious difficulties with the traditional cost accounting systems and to identify some of the questions that must be answered before managerially meaningful cost systems are developed. Because the JIT/ZI systems are just now being implemented in this country, the full impact of such systems on the accounting function is yet to be determined.

Notes

[1] Two authors have outlined the major problems facing the accounting function and factories when automated JIT/ZI processes are installed. An interested reader should examine Kaplan, Robert S., "Yesterday's Accounting Undermines Production," *Harvard Business Review*, July-August 1984, pp. 95-101 and Miller, Jeffrey M. and Thomas E. Vollmann, "The Hidden Factory," *Harvard Business Review*, September-October 1984, pp. 142-150.

[2] Miller, op. cit. p. 142.

[3] *Thor Power Tool Co. vs IRS Commissioner*, 439 US 522 (1979).

Total Responses General Questionnaire

Part I. Organization Characteristics

The following information is important for classifying the results of this survey:

1. The approximate number of organization employees. _____

2. Check (✔) the *one* category which *best* describes your organization:

   Manufacturing:

   Consumer   17.0%   (SIC Code _____)

   Industrial   47.7%   (SIC Code _____)

   Nonmanufacturing

   Healthcare _____

   Retailing   25.0%

   Utilities   _____

   Financial (banking, insurance, etc.) _____

   Other (please explain) Direct Mail 1.1%
   Wholesaler 6.8; Misc. 2.3%

3. The approximate annual dollar volume (revenues, sales, etc.) of your organization. _____

4. Internal inventory accounting method(s) is (are) used by your organization:

   a. LIFO   21.8%   Average Costs   4.6%

   b. FIFO   13.8%   LIFO & FIFO   17.2%

                           FIFO & Standard Costs   12.6%

   c. Standard Costs   25.3%   LIFO, FIFO Standard Costs   3.4%

   d. Other (please explain)   Actual Costs   1.1%

5. Are you considering a change in your inventory system?

   yes 11.6%   no 88.4% (If yes, please describe change.)

   _____

   _____

Part II. Inventory Management System(s) of the Organization

6. What type(s) of inventory management system(s) is (are) used for your organization's kinds of inventory?

Systems	Manufacturing			Service Parts	Supplies	Retailing	Other
	Raw Materials	Work-in-Process	Finished Goods				
a. Fixed-order quantity system	18.3%	11.0%	14.6%	12.2%	22.0%	8.6%	2.5%
b. Fixed time period	7.3	2.4	7.3	3.7	8.5	2.5	—
c. Materials Requirements Planning (MRP)	45.1	36.6	36.6	18.3	7.3	3.7	—
d. Distribution Requirements Planning (DRP)	1.2	2.4	15.9	2.4	1.2	9.9	1.2
e. Other (please identify or explain)	4.9	1.2	2.4	7.3	8.5	3.7	3.7

7. Is your inventory management system computer based?

     yes 77.3%   no 22.7% (If no, please skip to question 10.)

8. For which of the following are computer packages used? Please indicate as many as appropriate.

Decision Area	Designed In-House (Please check)	Software Package Brand Name and Vendor (if purchased)	Computer Hardware (Vendor and Model(s))
a. Bill of materials 54.8%	70.0%		
b. MRP 47.9%	60.0		
c. DRP 15.1%	81.8		
d. Master Scheduling 42.5%	70.9		
e. Inventory Mgt. 56.2%	67.5		
(1) Transaction History 80.8%	69.4		
(2) ABC Analysis 45.2%	66.6		
(3) Cycle Counting 45.2%	75.7		
(4) Multi-Locations 57.5%	69.0		
(5) Order Calculation 47.9%	74.2		
(6) Vendor Identification 61.6%	71.1		
(7) Purchase Order Preparation 52.1%	71.1		
f. Cost Accounting 67.1%	79.1		
g. General Ledger Accounting 75.3%	55.3		
h. Production Scheduling and Control 45.2%	79.4		
i. Forecasting 37.0%	81.4		
j. Other (please identify) 5.5%	50.0		

9. How would you characterize the software packages above?
   a. Unintegrated, standalone packages for most
      decision areas   28.8%.
   b. Modules that can stand alone or be integrated for
      most decision areas   43.8%
   c. Most decision areas totally integrated into single or
      separate packages   26.0%.
   d. Not applicable (please explain)   1.4%

10. Do you use an ABC inventory analysis?
    yes 43.5%   no 56.5%

11. Do you use quantity discounts in deciding how much to
    order yes 71.6%   no 28.4%

12. Do you use models in setting order quantities?

	Models		
	Formulas	Tables/ Nomographs	Experience	Other (Please Explain)
Raw Materials	25.7%	–	41.4%	–
Work-in-Process	20.0	–	18.8	–
Finished Goods	26.1	–	36.2	–
Service Parts	8.7	1.4	44.3	–
Merchandise Inventory	13.0	–	39.1	–
Supplies	10.1	–	52.9	–
Other	–	–	4.3	–

13. How do you establish your safety stock levels?

	Safety Stock Method		
	Formulas	Tables/ Nomographs	Experience	Other (Please Explain)
Raw Materials	21.5%	1.3%	43.0%	–
Work-in-Process	14.1	1.3	25.6	–
Finished Goods	21.3	1.3	42.5	–
Service Parts	11.3	–	45.0	–
Merchandise Inventory	10.0	–	43.8	–
Supplies	8.8	1.3	45.0	–
Other	–	–	–	–

14. For which of the following types of inventory are service level policies used?

Raw Materials	35.2%	Merchandise	
Work-in-Process	13.0	Inventory	35.2%
Finished Goods	53.7	Supplies	29.6
Service Parts	31.5	Other	—

15. Is the service level based on balancing carrying and stock out cost?

Raw Materials	22.2%	Merchandise	
Work-in-Process	11.1	Inventory	33.3%
Finished Goods	35.1	Supplies	13.9
Service Parts	19.4	Other	—

16. If you use a fixed-time period system, what fixed-time period is used for reviewing inventories and placing orders?

Raw Materials	One Week 26.9%
Work-in-Process	One Week 15.4
Finished Goods	One Week 23.1
Service Parts	Four Weeks 11.5
Merchandise Inventory	One Week 24.0
Supplies	Four Weeks 14.8
Other	—

17. How is the fixed-time period determined?

 a. Cost analysis 4.5%
 b. Organization review schedule 59.1%
 c. Other (please explain) Usage history 13.6%

18. Do you cycle count inventories? yes _____ no _____

Raw Materials	61.0%	Merchandise Inventory	30.5
Work-in-Process	40.7	Supplies	18.6
Finished Goods	57.6	Other	–
Service Parts	32.2		

If you use a Material Requirement Planning (MRP) inventory management system, please answer questions 19 through 24; otherwise, please skip to question 25 in Part III of the questionnaire.

19. What lot sizing rule do you use?

		Level Used		
		End		Raw
	Lot Sizing Rule	Item	WIP	Materials
a.	Lot for Lot	38.5%	23.1%	28.2%
b.	Economic Order Quantity	25.6	23.1	23.1
c.	Economic Review Period	7.7	5.1	12.8
d.	Part-Period Balancing	10.3	2.6	12.8
e.	Other (please identify or explain)			

20. Where is safety stock maintained?

a.	End Items	61.5%
b.	Work-in-Process	20.5
c.	Raw Materials	43.6
	(1) With Vendor	30.8
	(2) In-House	56.4
d.	Service Parts	35.9

21. What time buckets are used for exploding and time-phasing material requirements.?

    One week 62.9%; One month 20.0%
    (days/weeks/months)

22. How is the MRP generated?

    a. Net Change 38.2%
    b. Full regeneration 58.8

23. How often is the MRP operated or run?
    One Week 62.5%
    (days/weeks/months)

24. How would you characterize your MRP system?

    a. Class A system   8.1%
    b. Class B system   27.0
    c. Class C system   13.5
    d. Class D system   2.7
    e. Not certain   48.6

Part III. Inventory System
Performance Measures

25. Do you monitor inventory performance?
    yes 95.2%   no 4.8%

26. Which of the following measures are used as inventory performance standards?

Performance Standards	Raw Materials	Work-in-Process	Finished Goods	Service Parts	Aggregate or Total	Individual Items	Other (please identify)
a. Turnover	46.9%	29.6%	46.9%	14.8%	39.5%	23.5%	—
b. Lead times	22.2	12.3	24.7	11.1	3.7	18.5	—
c. Stockouts (or backorders)	12.3	1.2	25.9	11.1	3.7	11.1	—
d. No. of orders (or setups)	1.2	11.1	9.9	1.2	3.7	6.2	—
e. Optimum (or desired) levels	17.3	13.6	32.1	9.9	11.1	12.3	—
f. % of orders late	2.5	9.9	27.2	6.2	12.3	6.2	—
g. Obsolete inventory	27.2	25.9	34.6	11.1	16.0	17.3	—
h. Other (please identify)	1.2	1.2	1.2	—	1.2	—	—

Inventory Items

27. What method(s) is (are) used to derive these standards?
    a. Industry standards <u>13.9%</u>
    b. Experience <u>92.4%</u>
    c. Forecasted inventory needs <u>65.8%</u>
    d. Integrated business, output, and inventory planning <u>24.1%</u>
    e. Other (please explain) _____

28. How often are the performance measures <u>monitored?</u> (Note: if a measure is not monitored please indicate with N/A.)

Inventory Measure	Monitoring Frequency — Every: (days/weeks/months/quarters/years)
a. Turnover	Monthly 62.2%
b. Lead times	Not Applicable 53.7%
c. Stockouts (or backorders)	Not Applicable 43.9%
d. No. of orders (or setups)	Not Applicable 64.6%
e. Optimum (or desired) levels	Not Applicable 54.9%
f. % of orders late	Not Applicable 58.0%
g. Obsolete inventory	Monthly 32.1%
h. Other (please identify)	—

29. Who uses the inventory performance measures information?
    a. Accounting <u>83.1%</u>
    b. Materials Management <u>59.0%</u>
    c. Production Planners/Managers <u>54.2%</u>
    d. Plant Managers <u>57.8%</u>
    e. Finance <u>39.8%</u>
    f. Marketing <u>34.9%</u>
    g. Top Management <u>72.3%</u>
    h. Others (please explain) _____

Part IV. Respondent's Information

30. A small number of responding companies will be selected for a more thorough analysis of their inventory policies. Would you participate in such a field visit if chosen?

    yes 22.9%   no   77.1%

31. If you have specific graphs, tables, charts, formulas, etc. you would share with other readers of this report, please enclose copies with this questionaire. Your firm will not be identified.

32. Would you like a copy of the results of this survey?
    yes 67.5%   no   32.5%

33. The following information would be helpful to us. It will not be used as part of the report on this survey. If you prefer, you may simply leave any or all of the information blank.

Name _____

Title _____

Organization _____

Street Address _____

City _____State _____Zip Code _____

Name of Parent Company, if applicable. _____

Thank you. Your cooperation in completing this questionnaire is greatly appreciated.

Please return the completed questionnaire in the enclosed envelope to:

Charles D. Mecimore
James K. Weeks
School of Business and Economics
University of North Carolina at Greensboro
Greensboro, NC 27412-5001

919/379-5658

Total Responses
Just-In-Time Questionnaire

Part I. Organization Characteristics

The following information is important for classifying the results of this survey:

1. The approximate number of organization employees. _____

2. Check (✔) the *one* category which *best* describes your organization:

Consumer	21.1%	(SIC Code _____)
Industrial	78.9%	(SIC Code _____)

3. The approximate annual volume (revenues, sales, etc.) of your organization. _____

Part II. Just In-Time Implementation Questions

1. Do you have a Zero Inventory or Just-In-Time program?

    yes 27.3%   no 72.7% (If no, please skip to question 13.)

2. Please briefly describe the nature of your ZI/JIT program.

    _____

3. How long has your ZI/JIT program been implemented?

    _____ months/years.   26.3% ≤ One year
                             73.6 ≤ Two years
                             100.0% ≤ Three years

4. How would you characterize your manufacturing system(s) where the ZI/JIT program is being implemented?

    a. Low volume, job shop   31.6%

    b. High volume, discrete or repetitive plant   36.8%

    c. High volume, continuous or process plant   21.1%

    d. Other (please describe)   10.5%

_____

_____

_____

5. On a scale of 1 (low) to 10 (high), please rate your ZI/JIT program's progress along the road to achieving the following. (Note: please omit items that do not apply.) (Mean)

4.6 a. Improving the reliability of sales forecasts of finished goods.

5.9 b. Eliminating inactive product line items.

6.0 c. Designing products to enhance:

    5.9 (1.) Standardizing product designs;

    5.7 (2.) Modularizing product designs;

    5.5 (3.) Computer-aided design.

4.8 d. Minimizing engineering changes of existing product designs.

4.9 e. Performing value engineering of existing product designs.

6.7 f. Reducing setup times.

8.2 g. Improving flow through the plant by:

    6.0 (1.) Group technology;

    6.5 (2.) Dedicated lines;

    4.8 (3.) Computer-aided manufacturing.

6.7 h. Improving plant "housekeeping" and orderliness.

5.5 i. Increasing the automation of:

    5.2 (1.) Material handling;

    6.1 (2.) Setups;

    5.7 (3.) Operations;

    5.3 (4.) Inspection and error detection.

5.9 j. Improving preventive maintenance of equipment.

8.0 k. Reducing defects by:

    6.7 (1.) Establishing a vendor quality
        assurance program;

    6.8 (2.) Using statistical process control
        charts;

    5.9 (3.) Using error signaling devices.

7.8 l. Reducing lot sizes.

6.4 m. Smoothing realistic master production schedules.

6.7 n. Balancing the work load.

7.3 o. Increasing control through visibility.

6.6 p. Pulling (instead of pushing) work through the system.

7.4 q. Improving purchasing operations by:

    6.6 (1.) Developing reliable vendors;

    5.9 (2.) Establishing a vendor network;

    6.8 (3.) Using blanket purchase orders;

    6.1 (4.) Using "pull systems" releases
        for deliveries;

    5.4 (5.) Using value analysis;

    6.7 (6.) Reducing vendor lead times to
        approach just-in-time deliveries.

5.2 r. Improving the timeliness and accuracy of:

    5.3 (1.) Product costs;

    4.7 (2.) Budgets;

    6.4 (3.) Inventory-and production-related
        records, files, transactions and
        information.

8.0 s. Developing the human resources by:

    7.5 (1.) Educating and training the
        management staff as well as
        the operators;

    6.9 (2.) Using quality circles, suggestion
        systems, compensation schemes
        and other means to promote
        teamwork;

    6.8 (3.) Enlarging job designs to provide
        multi-functional, flexible operators.

6. On a scale of 1 (low) to 10 (high), how would you rate the importance of the following factors for successfully implementing your ZI/JIT program?

6.5 a. Reliable sales forecasts.
7.3 b. Produceable product designs.
6.9 c. Minimum setup times.
7.0 d. Flow layout.
6.0 e. "Housekeeping" discipline.
5.0 f. Automation of:
    6.2 (1.) Material handling;
    6.7 (2.) Setups;
    6.3 (3.) Operations;
    7.3 (4.) Inspection.
6.9 g. Preventive maintenance.
7.9 h. Zero defect operations.
8.1 i. Minimum lot sizes.
6.9 j. Statistical quality control.
7.7 k. Smoothed master schedules.
7.5 l. Balanced work loads.
7.6 m. "Pull" execution of schedules.
9.0 n. Reliable vendors:
    8.6 (1.) Zero defects;
    8.3 (2.) Minimum (approaching just-in-time)
        lead times;
8.4 o. Timely and accurate information.
7.1 p. Multi-function operators.
8.4 q. Education and training.
9.0 r. Top management support.
8.8 s. Supervisory management support.
8.8 t. Middle management support.
8.2 u. A "champion."
2.0 v. Other (please identify) _____
    _____

7. On a scale of 1 (low) to 10 (high), how would you rate the
   following:
   (Mean)

   8.5 a. Top management's view of the importance of your
           ZI/JIT program.
   8.4 b. Top management's commitment to and support of
           your ZI/JIT program.

8. For each of the characteristics below (a — e), state in Column II
   the current experience given your stage of ZI/JIT program

implementation. Then state in Column I the experience that you would expect if you were still using your system in existence previous to the ZI/JIT system. Finally, state in Column III what you expect to achieve in the future with your current ZI/JIT program. (Note: if you are unable to use absolute measures, please use percent improvement measures in Column II and III.)

		Base	Δ from Col.I	Δ from Col. II
		Column I	Column II	Column III
			Current	Future
		Pre JIT	Estimate	Estimate
a.	Inventory turnover			
	(1.) Raw materials	100%	63.9%	133.5%
	(2.) Work-in-process	100%	130.1	227.4
	(3.) Finished goods	100%	27.9	72.9
	(4.) Total	100%	75.7	154.7
b.	Days' on hand inventory	100%	-35.8	-58.2
c.	Average setup time	100%	-58.6	-78.8
d.	Average lot size			
	(days' use)	100%	-71.6	-85.8
e.	Defect rates			
	(1.) From vendors	100%	-42.0	-68.0
	(2.) Internally	100%	-39.7	-60.6

10. To what degree have the following benefits been achieved from your ZI/JIT program?

		Degree of Improvement			
		Little/			Very
	Benefit	None	Some	Much	Much
a.	Reduced inventory				
	(1.) Materials	11.1%	11.1%	33.3%	44.4%
	(2.) Work-in-process		16.7	27.8	55.6
	(3.) Finished goods	16.7	44.4	16.7	22.2
b.	Reduced safety stock				
	(1.) Materials		11.1	50.0	38.9
	(2.) Work-in-process		5.9	47.1	47.1
	(3.) Finished goods	17.6	23.5	29.4	29.4
c.	Reduced lead times	11.1	27.8	27.8	33.3
d.	Better quality	5.6	38.9	38.9	16.7

e. Better production
   scheduling   <u>16.7</u>   <u>16.7</u>   <u>50.0</u>   <u>16.7</u>
f. Improved plant
   efficiency   <u>16.7</u>   <u>27.8</u>   <u>27.8</u>   <u>27.8</u>
g. Improved morale   <u>16.7</u>   <u>33.3</u>   <u>38.9</u>   <u>11.1</u>
h. Improved coordination
   among sales, production
   and engineering   <u>11.1</u>   <u>55.6</u>   <u>16.7</u>   <u>16.7</u>
i. Improved competitive
   position   <u>5.6</u>   <u>38.9</u>   <u>33.3</u>   <u>22.2</u>

11. How much would you estimate it would cost to implement your ZI/JIT program to its present stage? An approximate estimate will be helpful. Please include costs of software, hardware, people, equipment, etc.

    Costs to date   \$ Mean = \$658,375
    Total anticipated costs   \$ Mean = \$1,833,727

12. List, in order of difficulty, major problems you encountered in installing your JIT approach.

    <u>Employee attitude/training = 55.6%</u>
    <u>System design/equipment = 22.2%</u>
    <u>Vendor relations = 22.2%</u>

13. If you do not have a JIT system, please indicate why:
    a. Not applicable   <u>21.8%</u>
    b. Cost/benefit not present   <u>7.3%</u>
    c. Not aware of system   <u>12.7%</u>
    d. Other, please specify   <u>58.2%</u>

Part III

14. A small number of responding companies will be selected for a more thorough analysis of their inventory policies. Would you participate in such a field study if chosen?

    Yes <u>41.2%</u>   No <u>58.8%</u>

15. Would you like a copy of the results of this survey?

    Yes <u>94.7%</u>   No <u>5.3%</u>

16. The following information would be helpful to us. It will not be used as part of the report on this survey. If you prefer, you may simply leave any or all of the information blank.

Name _____

Title _____

Organization _____

Street Address _____

City _____State _____Zip Code _____

Name of Parent Company, if applicable _____

Thank you. Your cooperation in completing this questionnaire is greatly appreciated. Please return the completed questionnaire in the enclosed envelope to:

> Charles D. Mecimore
> James K. Weeks
> School of Business and Economics
> University of North Carolina at Greensboro
> Greensboro, NC 27412-5001
> 919/379-5658

Techniques in Inventory Management and Control

Chapter Two — Inventory Functions, Costs, and Order Quantity Decision Approaches
Chapter Three — When to Order

Articles

Aggarwal, S.C., "A Review of Current Inventory Theory and Its Applications," *International Journal of Production Research*, No. 12, 1974, pp. 443-472.

Alsdurf, William H., "Improving Inventory Records Now Becoming More Important," *Hospital Financial Management*, June 1980, pp. 62, 63.

Banks, J. and C. L. Hottenstein, "Simplification of the Economic Order Quantity Equation," *Journal of Purchasing and Material Management*, Vol. 17, No. 2, Summer 1981, pp. 19-22.

Banks, Jerry and Russell G. Heikes, "A Technical Aid for EOQ Determination," *American Journal of Small Business*, Spring 1983, pp. 27-30.

Baker, R. C. and Naufel Vilcassim, "Continuous Review Price Change Inventory Model," *Production and Inventory Management*, Fourth Quarter 1983, pp. 67-72.

Blackstone, John H., Jr. and James F. Cox, "Inventory Management Techniques," *Journal of Small Business Management*, April 1985, pp. 27-33.

Bowers, Billy B., "Product Costing in the MRP Environment," *Management Accounting*, December 1982, pp. 24-27.

Burben, Jack N., "The Challenge of Managing Inventories," *American Production and Inventory Control Society 1978 Conference Proceedings*, pp. 879-897.

Burch, Earl E. and John M. Garris, "Lower Costs Through Work-in-Process Inventory Control," *Industrial Management*, May-June 1983, pp. 27-31.

"Buyers Keeping Inventories Tight," *Purchasing World*, March 1984, p. 44.

Copley, John W., "Inventory Planning in a Wholesale Business," *Virginia Accountant*, June 1983, pp. 13-19.

"Economic Order Quantity Simplified," *Industrial Distribution*, January 1975, pp. 62-64.

"Electronics Comparing Mover Assembly Line by Implementing Team Work Center," *Computerworld*, April 25, 1983, pp. 26-27.

Elfner, Eliot S., "EOQ Analysis Incorporates Price Break Parameters," *Industrial Engineering*, June 1983, pp. 18-20.

Fancher, Derrell O. and David B. Beasley, "Inventory Control: Cost Cutting Through EOQ," *Hospital Financial Management*, November 1981, pp. 36-39.

Fraser, Donald R. and Norman Gaither, "Inventory Reductions Not the Automatic Answer to Higher Interest Rates," *Financial Executive*, November 1982, pp. 38-41.

Fuerst, William L., "Small Businesses Get a New Look at ABC Analysis for Inventory Control," *Journal of Small Business Management*, July 1981, pp. 39-44.

Gerwin, Donald, "Do's and Don'ts of Computerized Manufacturing," *Harvard Business Review*, March-April 1982, pp. 107-116.

Gilbert, James P. and Richard J. Schonberger, "Inventory-Based Production Control Systems: A Historical Analysis," *Production and Inventory Management*, Second Quarter 1983, pp. 1-4.

Janson, Robert L., "Graphic Indicators of Operations," *Harvard Business Review*, November/December 1980, pp. 164-170.

Jesse, Richard R. Jr., Amitava Mitra and James F. Cox, "EOQ Formula: Is It Valid Under Inflationary Conditions," *Decision Sciences*, July 1983, pp. 370-374.

Johnson, Robert, "How Inventory Management Can Increase Profitability Dramatically," *National Public Accountant*, February 1982, pp. 22-24.

Jordan, Henry H., "How to Plan and Control Inventories," *Amercian Production and Inventory Control Society 1976 Conference Proceedings*, pp. 305-313.

Khan, Riaz, "MRP as a Scheduling System," *Industrial Management*, July-August 1982, pp. 12-17.

Krupp, James A. G., "Deterministic EOQ in a Production Environment," *Journal of Purchasing and Materials Management*, Summer 1983, pp. 24-30.

Lambert, Douglas and Robert Quinn, "Profit Oriented Inventory Policies Require a Documented Inventory Carrying Cost," *Business Quarterly (Canada)*, Autumn 1981, pp. 63-73.

Lingaraj, B. P., "Inventory Management in a Small Business," *Industrial*

Management, May-June 1982, pp. 21, 22.

Mitchell, C. R., R. A. Rappold and W. B. Faulkner, "An Analysis of Air Force EOQ Data with an Application to Reorder Point Calculation," *Management Science,* April 1983, pp. 440-446.

Ovellet, R., J. Roy, C. Cardinal and Y. Rosconi, "EOQ Applications in a Pharmaceutical Environment: A Case Study," *Journal of Operations Management,* Vol. 3, No. 1, November 1982, pp. 49-55.

Ramalengain, P., "Inventory Management: A Practical Approach to Boost Profit," *Industrial Management,* May-June 1981, pp. 18-23.

Saunders, Gary and Jeff Taylor, "Evaluating the Effect of Stockouts and Reorder Points on the EOQ," *Cost and Management (Canada),* March-April 1982, pp. 38-41.

Schwartz, Eli, "Excess Capacity in Utility Industries: An Inventory Theoretic Approach," *Land Economics,* February 1984, pp. 40-48.

Scott, John V., "Inventory Control . . . or Bust," *Cost and Management (Canada),* September-October 1981, pp. 26-32.

Singh, Harpal, "EOQ Calculations Plus Limited Order Cycles Help with Inventory Management," *Industrial Engineering,* June 1983, pp. 42, 44.

Sindey, Joseph F. Jr., "A Pedagogical Note on the EOQ Model," *Financial Review,* February 1983, pp. 111-113.

Taylor, Sam G. and Charles E. Bradley, "Optimal Ordering Strategies for Announced Price Increases," *Operations Research,* March/April 1985, pp. 312-325.

Wagner, H. M., "A Manager's Survey of Inventory and Production Control Systems," *Interfaces,* Vol. 2, 1972, pp. 31-39.

Welch, W. B., "Management's Role in Inventory Control," *Production and Inventory Management,* Vol. 20, No. 3, Third Quarter, 1979, pp. 85-94.

"With Pacific Metal's EDP . . . It's Inventory Full, Stock Turns Up," *Industrial Distribution,* May 1983, pp. 105-109.

Zenty, Thomas F. III., "ROP Discussion Helps EOQ Article," *Hospital Financial Management,* February 1982, p. 61.

Zimmerman, Gary W., "The ABC's of Vilfredo Pareto," *Production and Inventory Management,* Third Quarter 1975, pp. 1-9.

Zimmerman, H. J., "Periodic vs. Perpetual Inventory Control Systems," *Production and Inventory Management,* Vol. 7, No. 4, October 1966, pp. 66-79.

Chapter Four — Dependent Demand Inventory Systems

Anderson, J. C., R. S. Schroeder, S. B. Tupy and B. N. White "Material Requirements Planning Systems: The State of the Art," *Production and Inventory Management,* Vol. 23, No. 4, Fourth Quarter 1983, pp. 51-67.

Ball, C. Harish and Larry P. Ritzman, "An Empirical Investigation of Different Strategies for Material Requirements Planning," *Journal of Operations Management,* February 1983, pp. 67-77.

Baxter, John D., "Improved Controls Cut Through the Maze of Production Line Problems," *Iron Age,* February 20, 1984, pp. 42-51.

Benton, W. C., "Purchase Quantity Discount Procedures and MRP," *Journal of Purchasing and Materials Management,* Spring 1983, pp. 30-34.

Billington, Peter J., John O. McClain and L. Joseph Thomas, "Mathematical Programming Approaches to Capacity-Constrained MRP Systems: Review, Formulation and Problem Reduction," *Management Science,* October 1983, pp. 1126-1141.

Colman, Harry L., "Planning Brings MRP Success," *Data Management,* November 1983, pp. 24-27.

Chang, C. Alex, Larry G. Brown and L. Ray Johnson, "Analysis of Buffering Techniques in MRP Systems with a Matrix Loading Model," *IEE Transactions,* December 1983, pp. 305-312.

Corner, I. and A. Chapman, "MRP Systems: Using New Technology in Manufacturing," *Leadership and Organization Development Journal,* 1983, pp. 26-29.

Davenport, Frederick J,. "Financial Management Through MRP," *Management Accounting,* June 1983, pp. 26-29.

De Bolt, Marc A. and Luk N. Van Wassenhove, "Cost Increases Due to Demand Uncertainty in MRP Lot Sizing," *Decision Sciences,* July 1983, pp. 345-362.

De Bolt, Marc A. and Luk N. Van Wassenhove, "Lot Sizes and Safety Stocks in MRP: A Case Study," *Production and Inventory Management,* First Quarter 1983, pp. 1-16.

De Rose, Louis J., "Negotiating Lead Times with MRP," *Purchasing World,* February 1983, p. 70.

Edson, E. W. and R. A. Stahl, "MRP II/Case-in-Point EG & G Sealol," *Production and Inventory Management Review and APICS News,* Vol. 4, No. 3, March 1984, pp. 24-28, 57.

Etiemie, Eisenhower C., "MRP May Not Be Right For You: At Least Not Yet," *Production and Inventory Management,* Third Quarter 1983, pp. 33-46.

"Fuel Parts Maker Speeds Operations Via MRP," *Computerworld,* January 20, 1984, Special Report 32.

Gaither, Norman, "An Inproved Lot-Sizing Model for MRP Systems," *Production and Inventory Management,* Third Quarter 1983, pp. 10-20.

Glaza, Thomas L., "Assess Costs, Benefits Before Implementing MRP," *Computerworld,* April 25, 1983, Special Report 6, 10, 12.

Goddard, Walter E., "Kanban Versus MRP II - Which Is Best for You?" *Modern Materials Handling,* November 5, 1982, pp. 40-48.

Hanks, Dave, "Planning Systems vs. Manufacturing Control," *Computerworld,* April 25, 1983, Special Report 23.

Hartley, Kenneth, "How to Plan and Organize an MRP Project," *Production and Inventory Management,* First Quarter 1983, pp. 53-65.

Kropp, Dean H. and Robert C. Carlson, "A Lot-Sizing Algorithm for Reducing Nervousness in MRP Systems," *Management Science,* February 1984, pp. 240-244.

Kropp, Dean H., Robert C. Carlson and James V. Jucker, "Heuristic Lot-Sizing Approaches for Dealing with MRP System Nervousness," *Decision Sciences,* April 1983, pp. 156-169.

Kull, David, "MRP: The Industrial Revolution Meets the Information Age," *Computer Decisions,* October 1983, pp. 120-133,240.

Lasey, Thomas, "Merging Graphics with MRP," *Interface,* Summer 1983, pp. 17-19.

Lee, Raymon S., "Material Requirements Planning and the Organization," *Production and Inventory Management,* Third Quarter 1983, pp. 103-114.

"Manufacturer Boosts Efficiency with MRP II," *Computerworld,* April 25, 1983, Special Report 16.

"Manufacturer Fine Tunes Planning with MRP System," *Computerworld,* March 26, 1984, p. 40.

Macwilliam, Peter, "A Management Guide to Successful MRP Implementation," *Industrial Management (Canada),* May 1983, pp. 24-26, 63.

McGraw, John F. and John L. Daly, "Inventory Control: Should It Be Order Point or Material Requirements Planning," *Michigan CPA,* Spring 1982, pp. 23, 24.

Miller, J. G. and L. G. Sprague, "Behind the Growth in Materials Requirements Planning," *Harvard Business Review,* Vol. 53, September/October 1975, pp. 83-91.

"MRP Drives AS/RS - Cuts Inventory $12 Million/Teamwork Was the Key in Developing Our System," *Modern Materials Handling,* August 5, 1983, pp. 38-47.

"MRP II: A Framework for Factory Management," *Datamation*, February 1984, pp. 102-108.

"MRP II Gives Dramatic Savings in Labor and Inventory Costs," *Modern Materials Handling*, November 7, 1983, pp. 56-59.

Morello, Carmine D., "Successful MRP Needs Full-Time Project Leader," *Computerworld*, March 26, 1984, Special Report 30.

Nakane, Jinechiro and Robert W. Hall, "Management Specs for Stockless Production," *Harvard Business Review*, May-June 1983, pp. 84-91.

Nelson, Nancy S., "MRP and Inventory and Production Control in Process Industries," *Production and Inventory Management*, Fourth Quarter 1983, pp. 15-22.

Putman, Arnold O., "MRP for Repetitive Manufacturing Shops: A Flexible Kanban System for America," *Production and Inventory Management*, Third Quarter 1983, pp. 61-88.

Sarkissian, Geoffrey, "Planning Critical to Small Firms' MRP Success," *Computerworld*, April 25, 1983, Special Report 18, 24.

Schroeder, Roger G., Roger Gagnon, John C. Anderson, Sharon Tupy, and Edna M. White, "A Study of MRP Benefits and Costs," *Journal of Operations Management*, October 1981, pp. 1-9.

Schultz, T. R., "MRP to BRP: The Journal of the 80's," *American Production and Inventory Control Society 24th Annual International Conference Proceedings*, 1981, pp. 10-12.

Schull, Joseph S., "Computerized Planning Systems Marketing, Production, Other Functions," *Marketing News*, March 18, 1983, pp. 19-20.

Spencer, Michael S., "Planning Applications for MRP," *Production and Inventory Management*, Second Quarter 1983, pp. 52-62.

Swann, Don, "MRP: Is It a Myth or Panacea? Key to Answer Is Commitment of Management to It," *Industrial Engineering*, June 1983, pp. 34-40.

Thompson, Karen, "MRP II in the Repetitive Manufacturing Environment," *Production and Inventory Management*, Fourth Quarter 1983, pp. 1-14.

Thurston, Philip H., "Requirements Planning for Inventory Control," *Harvard Business Review*, May-June 1972, pp. 101-112.

Weeks, Peter, "Don't Miss the MRP Boat," *Management Accounting*, February 1983, pp. 40-41.

Weston, Frederick C. Jr., "The Process of Planning for MRP Incorporating a Systems Viewpoint," *Production and Inventory Management*, Second Quarter 1983, pp. 15-25.

White, Edna M., "Implementing an MRP System Using the Lewin-Schein Theory of Change," *Production and Inventory Management*, Vol. 21, No. 1,

First Quarter 1980, pp. 1-2.

Whiteside, David and Jules Arbose, "Unsnarling Industrial Production: Why Top Management Is Starting to Care," *International Management (UK)*, March 1984, pp. 20-26.

Williams, Joe L., Thomas R. Minnich, Freeman G Rohlfins and Alan P. Chmelewski, "Application of Manufacturing Resource Planning to Specialty Metals — A Batch Process Industry," *Production and Inventory Management*, Fourth Quarter 1983, pp. 51-66.

Chapter Five — Inventory Management Information Systems

Ahern, Bob, "Applying MRP II Principles to the Selection, Implementation of Manufacturing Software," *Computerworld*, April 25, 1983, Special Report 12, 13.

Arroyo, Julio B. Jr., "The New Scanners: Better MRP Through Bar Code," *Interface*, Autumn 1983, pp. 22-26.

Audit Approaches for a Computerized Inventory System, American Institute of Certified Public Accountants, 1980.

Arnold, C. T., R. W. Burke, and S. Cassriel, "The Micro Manufacturing Software Demesne," *Production and Inventory Management Review and APICS News*, Vol. 4, No. 1, January 1984, pp. 40-46.

"Bar Code Tech Monitors Honeywell Shop Floor," *Computerworld*, March 26, 1984, Special Report 14, 22.

Barger, Bruce and Larry Gould, "Computers — Where We're Going Tomorrow," *Modern Materials Handling*, November 21, 1983, pp. 42-50.

Bolt, Kevin N. and Larry P. Ritzman, "Irregular Workloads with MRP Systems: Some Causes and Consequences," *Journal of Operations Management*, August 1983, pp. 169-182.

Carbone, Tobias C., "Entrepreneur: Should You Compute?" *Management World*, June 1982, pp. 31-32.

Clifford, Robert and Anita Lans, "MRP Software Study-Methods for Evaluation," *Computerworld*, January 30, 1984, Special Report 47.

Cooke, James Aaron, "A Dynamic Approach to Distribution," *Traffic Management*, July 1983, pp. 55-58.

Dern, Daniel P., "The Start of a State of Mind," *Infosystems*, September 1983, pp. 18-20.

Elrick, Charles R., "Turnkey Accounting Systems," *Interface: Administrative and Accounting,* Autumn 1983, pp. 28-30.

Gand, Harvey and Milt E. Cook, "Choosing an MRP System," *Datamation,* January 1983, pp. 84-92.

Gray, Christopher, "Using MRP II to Get the Job Done," *Computer Data (Canada),* June 1983, pp. 6-7.

Grinnell, James E., "Distribution Resource Planning Systems Pick Up Where MRP Systems Leave Off," *Mini-Micro Systems,* November 1983, pp. 125-126.

Hayhow, Peter P., "Choosing the Right Manufacturing System/Quick Payoffs: The Key to Keeping Top Management Enthused," *Infosystem,* April 1983, pp. 48-54.

Hohenstein, C. L., "Microcomputer Spreadsheets for Inventory - A Schematic," *Production and Inventory Management Review and APICS News,* Vol. 4, No. 1, January 1984, pp. 26-28, 50.

Jacobs, F. Robert, "The OPT Scheduling System: A Review of a New Production Scheduling System," *Production and Inventory Management,* Third Quarter 1983, pp. 47-51.

Kahn, Arthur, "The Chicken and the Computer," *American Journal of Small Business,* Winter 1983, pp. 10-12.

"Large-Scale MRP Applications-Low Cost, Low Risk," *Data Management,* November 1983, pp. 28-29.

Meyer, David, "MRP Software Packages Bring Cost of MRP in Reach," *Computerworld,* April 25, 1983, Special Report 3, 6.

"Package Greases MRP for Oil Tools Company," *Computerworld,* November 7, 1983, p. 31.

Pinella, Paul, "Bargain Basement MRP," *Interface: Manufacturing and Engineering,* Spring 1983, pp. 12-14, 16-17.

Regan, Sean, John Harhen, Jim Browne, and M. E. J. O'Kelley, "The Design of a Microcomputer-Based Net Change MRP System," *Computers in Industry,* October 1983, pp. 243-252.

Ricker, Michael F., "Software: Information Modelling," *Small Systems World,* July 1983, p. 34.

Rushinck, Sara F., "Manufacturing Information Systems Using Computer Assisted Design (CAD), Computer Assisted Manufacturing (CAM) and Material Requirements Planning (MRP)," *Managerial Finance (UK),* 1983, pp. 6-7.

Schultz, H. K., "Microcomputers and Manufacturing, Distribution and Service Organizations," *Production and Inventory Management,* Vol. 24, No. 4, Fourth Quarter 1983, pp. 87-93.

"The Automated Warehouse—Billions to be Saved," *Modern Materials*

Handling, April 6, 1983, pp. 57-59.

Vollum, Robert B., "43 Ways Computers Can Help You," *Purchasing World,* June 1983, pp. 81-82.

Waliszewski, David, "The Decision Maker's Guide to MRP/Vendor Roundup: A Who's Who in Manufacturing Software," *Interface,* Autumn 1983, pp. 12-21, 36-39.

Walker, Dennis M. and Richard A. Wyck, "A Procedure to Determine the Least Cost Purchased-Part Planned Lead-Time for Items Controlled by an MRP System," *Computers and Industrial Engineering,* 1983, pp. 295-308.

Chapter Six — Measuring Inventory Management Effectiveness

Abelson, Harold R., "Research the Ratios — Primer #3, *Credit and Financial Management,* September 1982, p. 21.

Beed, Teresa, "Using Operating Cycle Figures to Spot Inventory and Accounts Receivable Problems," *Montana Business Quarterly,* Autumn 1981, pp. 23-26.

Bonsack, Robert A., "How to Use Ratios Effectively as an Inventory Control Measure," *Corporate Accounting,* Spring 1983, pp. 62-67.

Britney, Robert R., "Growth Product Lines and Realistic Inventory Turns," *International Journal of Physical Distribution and Materials Management (UK),* 1980, pp. 193-205.

Britney, Robert R., "Productivity and Inventory Turnovers: How High Is High Enough," *Business Quarterly (Canada),* May 1982, pp. 61-67, 74.

Broeren, Mary Ann, "Perspectives on Profit," *Retail Control,* September 1981, pp. 39-46.

Dudick, Thomas S., "How to Avoid Some Common Pitfalls in Accounting Inventory," *Practical Accountant,* November 1982, pp. 67-73.

Feinschreiber, Robert, "Techniques for Reducing Inventory Costs," *Taxes,* August 1982, pp. 617-620.

Finefrock, C.A., "Target Inventory Analysis: How to Determine 'How Much Inventory is Enough?'," *American Production and Inventory Control Society 23rd Annual Conference Proceedings,* 1980, pp. 104-107.

Hunt, C., "Inventory Management Measures in the Real World," *American Production and Inventory Control Society Planning and Control Seminar Proceedings,* March 1982, pp. 13-20.

Janson, Robert L., "Key Indicators for Production and Inventory Control," *American Production and Inventory Control Society 1981 Conference Proceedings,* pp. 319-321.

Jordan, H. H., "Inventory Budgets: Key to Profits and Growth," *American Production and Inventory Control Society 24th Annual International Conference Proceedings*, 1981, pp. 247-250.

Mitchell, Ralph C., III, and Richard J. Metzler, "The Second-Generation Management Audit," *Public Utilities Fortnightly*, May 12, 1983, pp. 21-25.

Pittiglio, Robin, Todd and McGrath Annual Study, "Inventory Performance for High Technology Industries - 1982," *Production and Inventory Management Review and APICS News*, Vol. 3, No. 6, pp. 27-31, 58.

Raedels, Alan R., "Measuring the Productivity of Materials Management," *Journal of Purchasing and Materials Management*, Summer 1983, pp. 12-18.

Reed, Seth O., "How to Measure Your Company's Performance," *Inc.*, August 1980, pp. 77-79.

Reisman, Arnold, "Material Management: The Need for a Systems Approach," *Hospital Material Management Quarterly*, November 1983, pp. 13-18.

Rivers, D. L., "ABC and Finished Goods," *Production and Inventory Management*, Vol. 23, No. 2, Second Quarter, 1983, pp. 5-11.

Silver, Alan, "What's Wrong with Stock Turns?," *Industrial Distribution*, May 1982, pp. 199-202.

Thor Power Tool Co. vs. IRS Commissioner, 439 US 522 (1979).

"Tracking Inventory," *Chain Store Age Executive*, July 1981, p. 91.

Warrington, Rosemary, "Measuring Inventory Return on Investment," *Retail Control*, January 1982, pp. 15-21.

Wheelwright, Steven C. and Robert H. Hayes, "Competing Through Manufacturing," *Harvard Business Review*, January-February 1985, pp. 99-109.

Chapter Seven — Zero Inventories Approach to Inventory Management

Brooks, Roger, "MRP: The Right Stuff for Just-In-Time," *Quality*, May 1985, p. 20.

Cole, Robert E., "Target Information for Competitive Performance," *Harvard Business Review*, May/June 1985, pp. 100-109.

Cook, James, "Kanban, American-Style," *Forbes*, October 8, 1984, pp. 66, 70.

Haynsworth, Hugh C., "A Theoretical Justification for the Use of 'Just-In-Time' Scheduling," *Production and Inventory Management*, First Quarter 1984, pp. 1-3.

Harbour, James E., "Just in Time, Not Just in Case," *Corporate Accounting*, Spring 1985, pp. 5-8.

"How Just-In-Time Inventories Combat Foreign Competition," *Business Week*, May 14, 1984, p. 176.

"Kanban Techniques Allow Printer Manufacturer's Daily Production to Quadruple," *Computerworld*, May 27, 1985, Special Report 18-19.

"Kanban: The Just-In-Time Japanese Inventory System," *Small Business Report*, February 1984, pp. 69-71.

Kull, David, "Manufacturing Systems: Can East Meet West?," *Computer Decisions*, October 1984, pp. 50-65.

Lorinez, James A., "Suppliers Question Approaches to JIT," *Purchasing World*, March 1985, pp. 74, 76, 82.

Manoochehri, G. H., "Improving Productivity with the Just-In-Time System," *Journal of Systems Management*, January 1985, pp. 23-26.

"MRP II and JIT Combat Waste in Manufacturing," *Modern Materials Handling*, June 1985, pp. 70-73.

Pegels, C. Carl, "The Toyota Production System — Lessons for American Management," *International Journal of Operations & Production Management (UK)*, Vol. 4, No. 1, 1984, pp. 3-11.

Priestman, Sarah, "SQC and JIT: Partnership in Quality," *Quality Progress*, May 1985, pp. 31-34.

Ritzman, Larry P., Barry E. Kiny and Lee J. Krajewski, "Manufacturing Performance — Pulling the Right Levers," *Harvard Business Review*, March/April 1984, pp. 143-152.

Sepehri, Mehran, "How Kanban System is Used in an American Toyota Motor Facility," *Industrial Engineering*, February 1985, pp. 50-56.

Spurgeon, Edward V., "Just-In-Time Implementation: Job Shop Versus Flow Shop," *Readings in Zero Inventory*, APICS 27th Annual International Conference, October 9-12, 1984, pp. 88-89.

Swartley-Loush, Judy, "Just-In-Time — Is It Right for You?," *Production Engineering*, June 1985, pp. 60-63.

Toyo Kogyo Co. Ltd. (A) and (B), Harvard Business School Cases Nos. 9-682-092 and 0-682-093, 1982.

Walters, Craig R., "Profit and Loss," *Inc.*, April 1985, pp. 109-111.

Wildermann, Horst, "Implementation Strategies for the Integration of Japanese Kanban-Principles in German Companies," *Engineering Costs & Production Economics (Netherlands)*, April 1985, pp. 305-319.

Williams, Jan "Just-in-Time Ideally Suited to Smaller Manufacturing Operations," *CPA Journal*, March 1985, pp. 81-83.

Chapter 8 — Implications of Future Inventory Systems for Accounting

"Cost Accounting: A Revolution in the Making," *Corporate Accounting,* Spring 1985, pp. 10-16.

Edwards, James B. and Julie A. Heard, "Is Cost Accounting the No. 1 Enemy of Productivity?," *Management Accounting,* June 1984, pp. 44-49.

Hunt, Rick, Linda Garrett, and Mike C. Merz, "Direct Labor Cost Not Always Relevant at H-P," *Management Accounting,* February 1985, pp. 58-62.

Johannson, Hank, "The Revolution in Cost Accounting," *Production and Inventory Management Review and APICS News,* January 1985, pp 42-46.

Kaplan, Robert S., "The Evolution of Management Accounting," *The Accounting Review,* July 1984, pp. 390-418.

Kaplan, Robert S., "Yesterday's Accounting Undermines Production," *Harvard Business Review,* July-August 1984, pp. 95-101.

Miller, Jeffrey G. and Thomas E. Vollmann, "The Hidden Factory," *Harvard Business Review,* September-October 1985, pp. 142-150.

Books

Atkinson, C., *Inventory Management for Small Computers,* New York: Dilithium Press, 1982.

Brown, R. G., *Decision Rules for Inventory Management,* New York: Holt, Rinehart & Winston, Inc., 1967.

Brown, R. G., *Statistical Forecasting for Inventory Control,* New York: McGraw-Hill Book Company, 1959.

Buffa, Edward, *Meeting the Competitive Challenge,* New York: Dow Jones-Irwin, 1985.

Buffa, E. S. and J. G. Miller, *Production - Inventory Systems: Planning and Control,* Third Edition, Homewood, Ill.: Richard S. Irwin, Inc., 1979.

Dees, Paul, *Production and Inventory Management in the Technological Age.* Englewood Cliffs, N.J.: Prentice-Hall, Inc., 1983.

Dieo, P., *Production and Inventory Management in the Technological Age,* Englewood Cliffs, N.J.: Prentice-Hall, Inc. 1983.

Fogarty, D. W. and T. R. Hoffman, *Production and Inventory Management,* Cincinnati: Southwestern Publishing Company, 1983.

Greene, J. H. (Ed.), *Production and Inventory Control Handbook*, New York: McGraw-Hill Book Company, 1970.

Hadley, G. and T. M. Whitien, *Analysis of Inventory Systems*, Englewood Cliffs, N.J.: Prentice-Hall, Inc., 1983.

Hall, Robert T., *Zero Inventories*, New York: Dow Jones-Irwin, 1983.

Hax, A. C. and D. Candea, *Production and Inventory Management*, Englewood Cliffs, N.J.: Prentice-Hall, Inc., 1984.

Jannis, C. Paul, Carl H. Poedtke, Jr. and Donald R. Ziegler, *Managing and Accounting for Inventories*, Third Edition, New York: John Wiley and Sons, 1980.

Koren, Y., *Computer Control of Manufacturing Systems*, New York: McGraw-Hill Book Company, 1983.

Lavery, K.R., W.D. Darlington and S.L. Meslin, *Effective Inventory Management*, Hamilton, Ontario: The Society of Management Accountants of Canada, 1985.

Orlicky, J., *Materials Requirements Planning*, New York: McGraw-Hill Book Company, 1974.

Peters, Thomas J. and Robert H. Waterman, Jr., *In Search of Excellence*, New York: Harper & Row, 1982.

Plossl, George W., *Manufacturing Control*, New York: Reston Publishing Company, 1973.

Tersine, R. J., *Materials Management and Inventory Systems*, New York: Elsevier North Holland, Inc., 1976.

Wright, O. W., *MRP II: Unlocking America's Productivity Potential*, Boston: CBI Publishing Company, 1981.

Wright, O. W., *Production and Inventory Management in the Computer Age*, Boston: CBI Publishing Company, Inc., 1974.

Glossary*

* *ABC Classification* — Classification of the items in an inventory in decreasing order of annual dollar volume or other criteria. This array is then split into three classes, called A, B, and C. Class A contains the items with the highest annual dollar volume, Class B contains the medium dollar volume items, and Class C contains the low-dollar volume items.

ABC Inventory Control — An inventory control approach based on the ABC classification.

Active Inventory — Covers raw material, work-in-process, finished products which will be used or sold within the budgeted period without extra cost or loss.

Aggregate Inventory — All the inventory including anticipation, fluctuation, cycle, and transportation stock.

Aggregate Inventory Management — Specifically planning the overall levels of inventory that will be required and making sure that the individual replenishment techniques execute this overall policy.

Anticipation Inventories — Additional inventory above basic pipeline stock to cover projected trends of increasing sales, planned sales promotion programs, seasonal fluctuations, plant shutdowns and vacations.

Application Package — A computer program or set of programs designed for a specific application.

Arrival Date — The date purchased material is due to arrive at the receiving site.

Assembly Parts List — A list of all parts (may include subassemblies) comprising a particular assembly, as used in the manufacturing process. Syn: blend formula, mix ticket.

Available Inventory — The on-hand balance minus allocations, reservations, backorders and (usually) quantities held for quality problems.

* *Available to Promise* — The uncommitted portion of a company's inventory or planned production.

Average Inventory — When demand and lot sizes are expected to be relatively uniform over time, the average is projected as one-half the average

---

Reprinted with permission, American Production & Inventory Control Society, Inc., APICS Dictionary, Fifth Edition, 1984.

187

lot size plus the reserve stock. Historically the average can be calculated as an average of several inventory observations taken over several historical time periods, e.g., period-ending inventories may be averaged. When demand and lot sizes are not uniform, the stock level vs. time can be graphed to determine the average.

Backflush — The deduction from inventory of the component parts used in an assembly or subassembly by exploding the bill of materials by the production count of assemblies produced.

Backorder — An unfilled customer order or commitment it is an immediate (or past due) demand against an item whose inventory is insufficient to satisfy the demand.

Bank — A quantity of materials which is awaiting further processing.

Bill of Material — A listing of all the subassemblies, parts and raw materials that go into a parent assembly showing the quantity of each required to make an assembly.

Bill of Material Processor — A computer program for maintaining and retrieving bill of material information.

Bill of Material Structuring — The process of organizing bills of material to perform specific functions.

Bin Location File — A file that specifically identifies the physical location where each item in inventory is stored.

Bin Tag — A type of perpetual inventory, designed for storeskeeping purposes, maintained at the storage area for each inventory item.

Book Inventory — An accounting definition of inventory units or value obtained from perpetual inventory records rather than by actual count.

Bucketed System — An MRP, DRP or other time-phased system in which all time-phased data are accumulated into time periods or "buckets."

Bucketless System — An MRP, DRP or other time-phased system in which all time-phased data are processed, stored, and displayed using dated records rather than defined time periods or "buckets."

Carrying Cost — Cost of carrying inventory usually defined as a percent of the dollar value of inventory per unit of time. Depends mainly on cost of capital invested as well as the costs of maintaining the inventory such as taxes and insurance obsolescence, spoilage, and space occupied.

Cost of Capital — Refers to the imputed cost of maintaining a dollar of capital invested for a certain period. The cost is normally expressed as a percentage and may be based upon factors such as the average expected return on alternative investments and current bank interest rate for borrowing.

Cycle — In inventory control, a cycle is often taken to be the length of time between two replenishment shipments.

Cycle Counting — A physical inventory-taking technique where inventory is counted on a periodic schedule rather than once a year.

Cycle Stock — One of the two main components of any item inventory, the cycle stock is the most active part, i.e., that which depletes gradually and is replenished cyclically when orders are received.

Economic Order Quantity (EOQ) — A type of fixed order quantity, which determines the amount of an item to be purchased or manufactured at one time to minimize the combined costs of acquiring and carrying inventory.

Expected Demand — The quantity expected to be withdrawn from stock during the lead time when usage is at the forecasted rate.

Expected Value — The average value which would be observed in taking an action an infinite number of times.

Fixed Interval Reorder System — A periodic reordering system where the time interval between orders is fixed, such as weekly, monthly or quarterly, but the size of the order is not fixed and orders vary according to usage since the last review.

Fixed Order Quantity — A lot sizing technique in MRP that will always cause planned order to be generated for a predetermined fixed quantity or multiples thereof if net requirements for the period exceed the fixed order quantity.

Fixed Order System — An inventory control where the size of the order is fixed, but the time interval between orders depends on actual demand. This system consists of placing an order of a fixed quantity (the reorder quantity) whenever the amount on hand plus the amount on order falls to or below a specified level (the order point or reorder point).

Fluctuation Inventory — Inventories that are carried as a cushion to protect against forecast error.

Handling Cost — The cost involved in handling inventory.

Hardware — 1. Such as nuts, bolts, washers, clips, etc. 2. In data processing, refers to the computer and its peripherals (cf. software).

Inventory — Items which are in a stock point or work-in-process and which serve to decouple successive operations in the process of manufacturing a product and distributing it to the consumer. Inventories may consist of finished goods ready for sale; they may be parts or intermediate items; they may be work-in-process, or they may be raw materials.

Inventory Control — The activities and techniques of maintaining the stock of items at desired levels, whether they be raw materials, work-in-process, or finished products.

Inventory File — A file containing the net quantity of all items normally maintained in inventory.

Inventory Investment — The number of dollars that are tied up in all levels of inventory.

Inventory Management — The branch of business management concerned with the planning and control of inventories.

Inventory Policy — A definite statement of the philosophy of management on inventories.

Inventory Position — On hand plus on order minus allocations, reservations and backorders.

Inventory Record — Often used as synonymous with item record. However, in some of the more advanced software, the inventory records contain primarily inventory data for a given item at a given location. They are subordinate to, and linked to, the master record for the item.

Inventory Shrinkage — Losses resulting from scrap, deterioration, pilferage, etc.

Inventory Tax — Taxes based upon the value of inventory on hand at a particular time.

Inventory Turnover — The number of times that an inventory turns over, or cycles during the year. One way to compute inventory turns over is to divide the average inventory level into the annual cost of sales.

Inventory Usage — The value or the number of units of an inventory item consumed over a period of time.

Inventory Valuation — The value of the inventory at either its cost or its market value.

Item — Any unique manufactured or purchased part or assembly, that is, end product, assembly, subassembly, component, or raw material.

Item Number — A number which serves to uniquely identify a product, component, or raw material.

Item Record — The "master" record for an item. Typically it contains identifying and descriptive data, control values (lead times, lot sizes, etc.) and may contain data on inventory status, requirements, and planned orders. Item records are linked together by bill of material records (or product structure records), thus defining the bill of material.

Just-in-Time — A logistics approach designed to result in minimum inventory by having material arrive at each operation just in time to be used. In the narrow sense, just-in-time refers to the movement of material so as to have only the necessary material at the necessary place at the right time.

Kanban — A method of just-in-time production which uses standard containers with a single card attached to each. It is a pull system in which work centers which use parts signal with a card that they wish to withdraw parts from feeding operations.

Lead Time Inventory — This is inventory which is carried on hand during the lead time period in simple inventory systems. The lead time inventory will be equal to forecasted usage during the replenishment lead time.

Lead Time Offset — A term used in MRP where a planned order receipt in one time period will require the release of that order in some earlier time period based on the lead time for the item.

Least Total Cost — A dynamic lot-sizing technique that calculates the order quantity by comparing the carrying cost and the set-up (or ordering) costs for various lot sizes and selects the lot where these are most nearly equal.

Level of Service — A measure of the demand that is routinely satisfied by inventory, e.g., the percentage of orders filled from stock or the percentage of dollar demand filled from stock.

Lot-for-Lot — A lot sizing technique in MRP which generates planned orders in quantities equal to the net requirements in each period.

Lot Size — The amount of a particular item that is ordered from the plant or a vendor.

Lot Size Inventory — Inventories which are maintained whenever quantity price discounts, shipping costs, or set-up costs, etc. make it more economical to purchase or produce in larger lots than are needed for immediate purposes.

Lot Sizing — The process of, or techniques used in, determining lot size.

Lumpy Demand — A demand pattern with large fluctuations from one time period to another.

Management Information System — A manual or computerized system which anticipates the wide use of data for management planning and control purposes. Accordingly, the data are organized in a database and are readily available to a variety of management functions.

Manufacturing Resource Planning (MRP II) — A method for the effective planning of all resources of a manufacturing company. Manufacturing Resource Planning is a direct outgrowth and extension of closed-loop MRP.

Master Production Schedule (MPS) — For selected items, it is a statement of what the company expects to manufacture. It is the anticipated build schedule for those selected items assigned to the master scheduler.

Material Requirements Planning (MRP) — A set of techniques which uses bills of material, inventory data, and the master production schedule to calculate requirements for materials. It makes recommendations to release replenishment orders for material. Further, since it is time-phased, it makes recommendations to reschedule open orders when due dates and need dates are not in phase. Originally seen as merely a better way to order inventory, today it is thought of as primarily a scheduling technique, i.e., a method for establishing and maintaining valid due dates on orders.

Maximum Reasonable Demand — (During lead time) the sum of the expected demand and an allowance for protection against the uncertainty inherent in any forecast. The allowance for error is the product of the safety factor and the standard deviation of the errors in forecasting over a lead time. That is, Maximum Reasonable Demand = Expected Demand + (Safety Factor x Standard Deviation).

Mean Absolute Deviation (MAD) — The average of the absolute value of the deviations of some observed value from some expected value.

Microcomputer Processor — A special purpose "computer-on-a-chip" designed to control or monitor a specific purpose.

Minicomputer — A small, programmable, general-purpose computer often used for dedicated application or for distributed processing.

Min-Max System — A type of order point replenishment system, used on a fixed-interval, period review basis. The "min" is the order point, and the "max" is the "order-up-to" inventory level. The order quantity is variable, and is the result of the "max" minus available and on order inventory (when the latter are below the "min").

MRP II — See: manufacturing resource planning.

Net Requirements — In MRP, the net requirements for a part or an assembly are derived as a result of netting gross requirements against inventory on hand and the scheduled receipts. Net requirements, lot sized and offset for lead time, become planned orders.

Nomogram — A computational aid consisting of two or more scales drawn and arranged so that the results of calculations may be found by the linear connection of point on them. Often used for calculating economic lot sizes.

Obsolescence — Loss of product value resulting from a model or style change or technological development.

On-Hand Balance — The quantity shown in the inventory records as being physically in stock.

Opportunity Cost — The return on capital that could have resulted had the capital been used for some purpose other than its present use. Sometimes refers to the best alternative use of the capital and at other times to the average return from feasible alternatives.

Order Point — The inventory level such that if the total stock on hand plus on order falls to or below the order point, action is taken to replenish the stock. The order point is normally calculated as: forecasted usage during the replenishment lead time plus safety stock.

Ordering Cost — In calculating economic order quantities, refers to the costs which increase as the number of orders placed increases. Includes costs related to the clerical work of preparing, issuing, following and receiving orders, the physical handling of goods, inspections, and machine set-up costs, if the order is being manufactured. Syn: acquisition cost.

Past Period Balancing (PPB) — A dynamic lot sizing technique that uses the same logic as the Least Total Cost method. The difference is that PPB employs a routine called "Look Ahead/Look Back." When the Look Ahead/Look Back feature is used, a lot quantity is calculated and before it is firmed up, the next or the previous periods' demands are evaluated to verify whether it would be economical to include them in the current lot.

Percent of Fill — A measure of the effectiveness with which the inventory management system responds to actual demand. The percent of customer orders filled off the shelf can be measured in either units or dollars.

Period Order Quantity — A lot sizing technique under which the lot size will be equal to the net requirements for a given number of periods (e.g., weeks) into the future.

Periodic Order System — See: fixed interval reorder system.

Perpetual Inventory — Usually used to describe an inventory record-keeping system where each transaction in and out is recorded and a new balance is computed.

Perpetual Inventory Record — A computer record or document on which each inventory transaction is posted so that a current record of the inventory is maintained.

Physical Inventory — The determination of inventory quantity by actual count. Physical inventories can be taken on a continuous, periodic, or annual basis.

Pipeline Stock — The amount of stock held between the point where it is made and the point where it is used.

Post-Deduct Inventory Transaction Processing — A method of doing inventory bookkeeping where the book (computer) inventory of components is reduced only after completion of activity on their upper level parent or assembly.

Pre-Deduct Inventory Transaction Processing — A method of doing inventory bookkeeping where the book (computer) inventory of components is reduced prior to issue, at the time a scheduled receipt for their parent or assembly is created.

Probability — Mathematically, a number between 0 and 1 that estimates the fraction of experiments (if the same experiment were being repeated many times) in which a particular result would occur.

Probability Distribution — A table of numbers or a mathematical expression which indicates the frequency with which each of all possible results of an experiment should occur.

Processor Program — A software program used to convert computer instructions written in symbolic language into absolute language.

Procurement Lead Time — The time required by the buyer to select a supplier, and to place and obtain a commitment for specific quantities of material at specified times.

Product Structure — The way components go into a product during its manufacture. A typical product structure would show, for example, raw material being converted into fabricated components, components being put together to make subassemblies, subassemblies going into assemblies, etc.

Product Structure Record — A computer record defining the relationship of one component to its immediate parent and containing fields for quantity required, engineering efficiency, scrap factor, application selection switches, etc.

Purchasing Lead Time — The total lead time required to obtain a purchased item. Included here are procurement lead time, vendor lead time, transportation time, receiving, inspection, and put-away time.

Raw Material — Purchased items which are converted via the manufacturing process into components and/or products.

Real-Time Data Processing — The processing of transactions as they occur rather than batching them.

Regeneration MRP — An MRP processing approach where the master production schedule is totally re-exploded down through all bills of material at least once per week to maintain valid priorities. New requirements and planned orders are completely "regenerated" at that time.

Reorder Point — See: Order point.

Reorder Quantity — In a fixed order system of inventory control, the fixed quantity which should be ordered each time the available stock (on hand plus on order) falls below the order point. However, in a variable reorder quantity system, the amount ordered from time period to time period will vary.

Requirements Explosion — A method of calculating future demand for an item. Future production quantities are multiplied by the quantity in the bill of material. The results represent future demand.

❡ *Review Period* — The time between successive evaluations of inventory status to determine whether or not to reorder.

Safety Capacity — The planning or reserving for excess manpower and equipment above known requirements for unexpected demand. This reserve capacity is in lieu of safety stock.

Safety Stock — 1. In general, a quantity of stock planned to be in inventory to protect against fluctuations in demand and/or supply. 2. The average amount of stock on hand when a replenishment quantity is received.

Safety Time — In an MRP system, material can be ordered to arrive ahead of the requirement date. The difference between the requirement date and the planned in-stock date is safety time.

Sawtooth Diagram — A quantity vs. time graphic representation of the order point/order quantity inventory system showing inventory being received and then used up and reordered.

Seasonal Inventory — Inventory built up in anticipation of a peak season in order to smooth production (e.g., anticipation inventories).

Service vs. Investment Chart — A curve showing the amount of inventory that will be required to give various levels of customer service.

Setup Cost — The out-of-pocket costs associated with a machine setup (order) that would increase or decrease if the number of setups (orders) were increased or decreased.

Shelf Life — The amount of time an item may be held in inventory before it becomes unusable.

Shortage Cost — The marginal profit that is lost when a customer orders an item but it is not immediately available in stock.

Shrinkage — Reductions of material quantities of items in stock, in process, in transit. The loss may be caused by scrap, theft, deterioration, evaporation, etc.

Simulation — The technique of utilizing representative or artificial data to reproduce in a model various conditions that are likely to occur in the actual performance of a system. Frequently used to test the behavior of a system under different operating policies.

Slow Moving Items — Those inventory items with a low turnover, i.e., an item in inventory which has a relatively low rate of usage compared to the normal amount of inventory carried.

Software — The programs and documentation necessary to make use of the computer.

Source Program — A computer program written in symbolic language which will be converted into an absolute language object program using a processor program.

Standard Deviation — A measure of dispersion of data or of a variable.

Stock — Stored products or service parts ready for sale as distinguished from stores which are usually components or raw materials.

Stockkeeping Unit (SKU) — An item at a particular geographic location.

Stock Order — A manufacturing order to replenish stock as opposed to a production order to make a particular product for a specific customer.

Stockout — The lack of materials or components which are needed to be on hand in stock.

Stockout Percentage — A measure of the effectiveness with which the inventory management system responds to actual demand. The stockout percent can be a measurement of total stockouts to total line item orders, or of line items incurring stockouts during a period total line items are in the system.

Stores — Stored materials used in making a product.

Supplies — Materials used in manufacturing which are not normally charged to the finished production, such as cutting and lubrication oils, machine repair parts, glue, tape, etc.

Target Inventory Level — The equivalent of the "maximum" in a min-max system. The target inventory is equal to the order point plus the order quantity. It is often called an "order up to" inventory level and is used in a periodic review system.

Terminal — A remote input or output unit which is directly connected to a computer.

Time Phased Order Point (TPOP) — MRP for independent demand items. Gross requirements come from a forecast, not via explosion. This technique can be used to plan warehouse inventories as well as planning for service (repair) parts since MRP logic can readily handle items with dependent demand, independent demand or a combination of both.

Time Phasing — The technique of expressing future demand, supply and inventories by time period. Time phasing is one of the key elements of material requirements planning.

TPOP — Abbreviation for time phased order point.

Trigger Level — See: order point

Turnover — The number of times inventory is replaced during a time period; in other words, a measurement of investment inventory to support a given level of sales. It is found by dividing the cost of goods sold for the period by the average inventory for the period.

Two-Bin System — A type of fixed order system in which inventory is carried in two bins. A replenishment quantity is ordered when the first bin is empty. When the material is received, the serve bin is refilled and the excess is put into the working bin. This term is also used loosely to describe any fixed order system even when physical "bins" do not exist.

Unit Cost — Total labor, material, and overhead cost for one unit of production, i.e., one part, one gallon, one pound.

Unit Price — The price for each unit.

Vendor Lead Time — The time that normally elapses between the time an order is received by a supplier and his shipment of the material.

Vendor Measurement — The act of measuring the vendor's performance to the contract. Measurements usually cover delivery, quality, and price.

Zero Inventories — A philosophy of manufacturing based on planned elimination of all waste and on consistent improvement of productivity. It encompasses the successful execution of all manufacturing activities required to produce a final product, from design engineering to delivery and including all stages of conversion from raw material onward. The primary elements of zero inventories are to have only the required inventory when needed; to improve quality to zero defects; to reduce lead times by reducing setup times, queue lengths, and lot sizes; and to incrementally revise the operations themselves to accomplish these things at minimum cost. In the broad sense it applies to all forms of manufacturing, job shop and process as well as repetitive.

National Association of Accountants Committee on Research, 1986-87